EDINBURGH TRAVEL GUIDE 2025

A Local's Navigator to the Royal Mile, Whisky Tours, and Unforgettable Scottish Adventures

LUCAS BELLAVITA

COPYRIGHT

Copyright © 2025
LUCAS BELLAVITA]

All rights reserved. No part of this publication may be reproduced, distributed, or transmitted in any form or by any means, including photocopying, recording, or other electronic or mechanical methods, without the prior written permission of the publisher, except in the case of brief quotations embodied in critical reviews and certain other noncommercial uses permitted by copyright law.

DISCLAIMER

The information provided in this "EDINBURGH TRAVEL GUIDE 2025" is intended for general informational purposes only and is compiled from sources believed to be reliable. However, the author and publisher make no representations or warranties of any kind, express or implied, about the completeness, accuracy, reliability, suitability, or availability with respect to the information, products, services, or related graphics contained in this guide for any purpose. Any reliance you place on such information is therefore strictly at your own risk.

The author and publisher shall not be liable for any loss or damage including without limitation, indirect or consequential loss or damage, or any loss or damage whatsoever arising from loss of data or profits arising out of, or for, the use of this guide.

Table of Contents

06 **INTRODUCTION**

10 **CHAPTER 1**
Essential Preparations & Safe Travels

21 **CHAPTER 2**
The Royal Mile & Old Town Treasures

31 **CHAPTER 3**
Whisky Trails & Spirited Adventures

39 **CHAPTER 4**
Highland & Lowland Escapes

51 **CHAPTER 5**
A Taste of Scotland

CHAPTER 6 60
Museums & Historical Narratives

CHAPTER 7 65
Cultural Celebrations & Festive Spirit

CHAPTER 8 73
Hidden Gems & Quirky Finds

CHAPTER 9 80
Exploring Scotland's Natural Wonders

CHAPTER 10 86
Responsible Travel & Lasting Memories

CONCLUSION 93

ESSENTIAL MAPS 96

WELCOME TO EDINBURGH

INTRODUCTION

Let's picture this: a crisp autumn evening in Edinburgh. The kind where the air is sharp, carrying the scent of woodsmoke and damp stone. I'm standing on Calton Hill, the city spread out below me like a storybook illustration. The castle, a dark silhouette against the fading light, the winding streets of the Old Town, the elegant sweep of the New Town – it's all there, a living, breathing history. You know that feeling, right? That sense of being somewhere truly special, where every cobblestone has a tale to tell? That's the feeling I want you, and everyone who picks up this guide, to experience.

It's funny, my first time in Edinburgh wasn't exactly planned. I was backpacking through Europe, chasing a vague idea of adventure, and found myself on a late-night bus, shivering and slightly lost, heading north. I'd heard stories, of course – the castle, the festivals, the whisky – but nothing prepared me for the reality. I remember walking the Royal Mile, the ancient buildings looming on either side, feeling like I'd stepped into a different century. I stumbled into a tiny pub, the kind with low ceilings and warm, amber light, and found myself surrounded by locals, their accents thick and welcoming. They shared stories, poured me a dream of something smoky and potent, and made me feel like I'd found a home away from home.

That's what Edinburgh does, you see. It pulls you in, wraps you in its history and its heart, and leaves you wanting more. It's not just a city; it's an experience. And that experience, that feeling of connection, is what I want to share with you in this guide. This isn't just a list of places to see; it's a conversation, a friendly nudge in the right direction, a local's whispered secrets about the best pubs, the hidden gardens, the stories behind the stones.

You're holding this book because you're drawn to Edinburgh, just like I was. Maybe you're fascinated by the history, eager to walk the same streets as Mary Queen of Scots. Or maybe you're looking for adventure, ready to explore the Highlands and taste the whisky that's made Scotland famous. Perhaps you just want to experience the magic of a city that feels both ancient and alive. Whatever your reason, you're in the right place.

This guide is more than just practical information; it's a

Journey. We'll walk the Royal Mile together, exploring the closes and wynds that most tourists miss. We'll venture beyond the city, into the breathtaking landscapes of the Highlands and Lowlands. We'll taste the food, listen to the music, and learn the stories that make Scotland so unique. We'll talk about the best way to get a local SIM, and what to buy for your friends and family back home. We will also talk about the best places to eat in each city we explore.

And yes, we'll talk about whisky. Because no trip to Scotland is complete without a dram or two. We'll explore the distilleries, learn about the different regions, and discover the stories behind this iconic spirit. But we'll also talk about the people, the culture, the little things that make Edinburgh, and Scotland, so special.

Think of me as your friend in Edinburgh, the one who knows all the best spots and can help you avoid the tourist traps. I'll share my favorite pubs, my secret viewpoints, and the stories that make this city come alive. I'll give you practical advice, like how to navigate public transport and where to find the best haggis, but I'll also encourage you to slow down, to wander, to get lost in the moment.

Because Edinburgh isn't just a destination; it's a feeling. It's the sound of bagpipes echoing through the streets, the warmth of a pub fire on a cold night, the breathtaking views from Arthur's Seat. It's the stories you'll hear, the people you'll meet, and the memories you'll make.
 So, let's begin this adventure together. Let's explore the heart of Scotland, one cobblestone street, one whisky dram, one unforgettable moment at a time. Welcome to Edinburgh. Welcome to your Scottish adventure.

SCOTT MONUMENT

CHAPTER 1
ESSENTIAL PREPARATIONS & SAFE TRAVELS

It started with a postcard. A simple thing, really – a faded image of a stone circle silhouetted against a stormy Scottish sky. No message, no return address, just a date scribbled in the corner: "Samhain, 2025." I found it tucked between the pages of an old journal, a journal I hadn't opened in years. The journal belonged to my grandfather, a man who'd always held Scotland close to his heart, a man who'd vanished, seemingly without a trace, years ago. He had always told me stories of Scotland, its ancient stones and its mysterious lochs. He said the land held secrets, whispers of forgotten times. That

postcard, that date, it felt like a breadcrumb, a hint of something he wanted me to find. It felt like a call.

That's how this journey began. Not with a guidebook or a carefully laid plan, but with a question, a mystery that pulled me towards Scotland like a tide. It wasn't just about exploring a new place; it was about tracing a ghost, about finding answers in the echoes of the past. And I knew, deep down, that Samhain 2025 – Halloween, as most know it – was significant.

So, here I am, sharing the practicalities of travel, the things you need to know before you set foot on Scottish soil, but with a different kind of urgency. Because this isn't just about seeing the sights; it's about understanding the soul of a land, a soul that holds onto its secrets like a tightly clutched stone.

First, let's talk timing. You're coming in 2025, which means you're planning ahead, a smart move. Scotland's weather is… well, let's just say it's a character. It can shift from sunshine to a downpour in the time it takes to say "och." Packing layers is your best friend. A good waterproof jacket, sturdy boots, and a warm scarf are non-negotiable. If you're coming around Samhain, be prepared for shorter days and colder temperatures, but also for a unique atmosphere. The veil between worlds is said to be thin then, and you might just feel a different kind of magic in the air.

Visas? Depending on where you're coming from, you might need one. Check the UK government website for the most up-to-date information. Don't leave this to the last minute; bureaucracy can be a slow beast. Currency is the British pound, and while cards are widely accepted, having some cash on hand is always a good idea, especially in smaller towns.

Now, staying connected. A local SIM card is essential. You'll want to be able to access maps, translate phrases, and share your adventures with those back home. Look for providers with good coverage in the areas you'll be visiting. Cell phone reception can be spotty in the Highlands, so don't rely solely on your phone for directions when venturing into remote areas.

Safety. Scotland is generally a safe country, but like any destination, it pays to be aware. Keep an eye on your belongings, especially in crowded tourist areas. Be mindful of your surroundings, especially at night. And if you're planning on hiking or exploring remote areas, let someone know your plans and carry a map and compass.

But safety isn't just about avoiding pickpockets. It's also about respecting the culture. Scotland has a rich history and a strong sense of identity. Learn a few basic Gaelic phrases – even just "hello" (failte) and "thank you" (tapadh leat) – and you'll find people are more open and welcoming. Don't be afraid to ask questions, but be respectful of local customs and traditions.

And speaking of traditions, pay attention to the land. Scotland's landscape is breathtaking, but it's also fragile. Tread lightly. Leave no trace. Pack out what you pack in. Support local businesses, eat at family-owned restaurants, and buy from independent shops. You'll not only be helping the local economy, but you'll also be getting a more authentic experience.

Here's a tip most guidebooks miss: talk to people. Strike up conversations in pubs, cafes, and shops. You'll hear stories you won't find anywhere else. You'll learn about the hidden gems, the places locals love, the tales that have been passed down through generations. And as you travel, keep your eyes open for signs, symbols, anything that feels out of place. My grandfather always said Scotland speaks to those who listen. I don't know what I'm looking for, but I know it's there, hidden in the stones, whispered in the wind.

This journey isn't just about seeing Scotland; it's about understanding it. It's about feeling the weight of its history, the pull of its legends. It's about finding the answers that lie beneath the surface, the secrets that are waiting to be uncovered. And who knows? Maybe, just maybe, you'll find a piece of your own story along the way.

Remember that Scotland is a place of stories. The land is alive with them. Each stone, each loch, each ancient ruin whispers of a time long past. Take the time to listen. Learn the tales of the clans, the myths of the faeries, the legends of the heroes. Let the stories seep into your soul, and you'll find that Scotland isn't just a place you visit; it's a place you become a part of.

And as you prepare, consider this: what are you looking for?

What draws you to Scotland? Is it the history, the landscapes, the whisky? Or is it something more, something you can't quite put into words? Whatever it is, embrace it. Let it guide you. And be prepared to be surprised. Because Scotland has a way of revealing its secrets to those who are willing to look.

This is more than a trip. It's a quest. And as you pack your bags and prepare to step onto Scottish soil, remember that you're not just a tourist; you're a traveler, an explorer, a seeker. And who knows what you might find?

Alright, let's get down to the brass tacks of planning your Scottish adventure, the kind of information that turns a vague idea into a solid, exciting trip. We're talking about the groundwork, the stuff that ensures you're not caught off guard when you land, and that you're ready to embrace everything Scotland throws your way.

by a fire, autumn and winter have their own unique draw. The light is different, more golden, and the landscapes take on a brooding beauty. Just be prepared for shorter daylight hours and cooler temperatures. And if you have that postcard date in mind, Samhain 2025, you are looking at late October/early November, and that is a truly unique time to be there.

First, let's talk about timing. You've got 2025 in your sights, which is excellent. That gives you breathing room to really tailor your experience. Scotland, as you'll quickly learn, changes dramatically with the seasons. If you're after those long, bright days where the Highlands stretch out in all their glory, consider May to September. That's when you'll find the warmest temperatures, though 'warm' is a relative term. Be ready for sudden showers, even then. If you're a fan of dramatic landscapes and cozy evenings

15

Visas, that's the next hurdle. Check the official UK government website, and do it early. Rules change, and you don't want to be scrambling at the last minute. Depending on your nationality, you might need a visa, and those things take time. Get your paperwork in order, and you'll be one step closer to your Scottish adventure.

Currency is the British pound, and while cards are widely accepted, especially in cities and tourist areas, don't rely on them exclusively. Small shops, rural pubs, and some attractions might prefer cash. It's always a good idea to have a mix. ATMs are plentiful in towns and cities, but less so in the Highlands and islands.

Now, staying connected. You'll want a local SIM card, trust me. It makes life easier. You can pick one up at the airport or in any phone shop in a city. Look for providers with good coverage across Scotland. You'll need it for maps, translations, and staying in touch. Public Wi-Fi is available in many cafes and hotels, but it's not always reliable.

- Consider downloading offline maps before you go.
- Check if your phone plan has international roaming options, but a local SIM is usually cheaper.
- A portable power bank is a lifesaver, especially on long days out exploring.

Safety is paramount. Scotland is generally a safe place, but common sense applies. Keep an eye on your belongings, especially in crowded areas. Be aware of your surroundings, particularly at night. If you're hiking or exploring remote areas, tell someone where you're going and when you expect to be back.

- Emergency number in the UK is 999.
- Learn a few basic phrases in Gaelic.
- Respect local customs and traditions.

And speaking of respect, let's talk etiquette. Scotland has a rich cultural heritage, and it's important to be mindful of that. Scots are generally friendly and welcoming, but they appreciate it when visitors make an effort to understand their culture.

- Don't be afraid to ask questions, but do so politely.
- Learn about the history of the clans and the Highlands.
- Be respectful of ancient sites and monuments.

When you start traveling between cities, here is what to keep in mind, as if you were having a conversation with a fellow traveler.

Okay, so let's say you are in Edinburgh, and you want to see Glasgow. Getting there is easy. Trains run frequently, and it's about an hour's journey. You can also take a bus, which is usually cheaper but takes a bit longer. Once you're in Glasgow, there's plenty to do.

- Explore the Kelvingrove Art Gallery and Museum.
- Wander through the Merchant City.
- Check out the street art scene.

For places to stay, Glasgow has everything from budget hostels to luxury hotels. If you want a central location, look for places near the city center. Food-wise, you've got to try a proper Glasgow curry. It's a local favorite. And, of course, there's always the pubs, where you can sample some local beers and whiskies.

If you are looking to travel to Inverness from Edinburgh, you can take a train or bus, but I'd recommend renting a car if you want to explore the Highlands. It's a bit more expensive, but it gives you the freedom to stop wherever you want. Inverness is the gateway to the Highlands, and there's so much to see.

- Visit Loch Ness.
- Explore the Cairngorms National Park.
- Take a boat trip on the Moray Firth.

Inverness has a range of accommodation options, from cozy bed and breakfasts to grand hotels. For food, try some local seafood or game. And don't forget to sample some Highland whiskies.

Traveling to Aberdeen from Edinburgh is also best done by train, or you can drive. Aberdeen has a different vibe than Edinburgh or Glasgow. It's known as the Granite City, and it has a strong maritime history.

- Visit the Maritime Museum.
- Explore Old Aberdeen.
- Take a walk along the beach.

Aberdeen has a good selection of hotels and restaurants. For food, try some fresh seafood or some of the local beef. And, of course, there are plenty of pubs where you can try some local beers.

When you travel, be open to new experiences. Talk to locals, try new foods, and don't be afraid to get off the beaten path. That's where you'll find the real Scotland. And as you travel, remember to be respectful of the environment and the people you meet. Leave no trace, and support local businesses.

Remember, this trip is yours. Make it your own. Let Scotland surprise you. And most of all, enjoy the adventure.

EDINBURGH

CHAPTER 2
THE ROYAL MILE & OLD TOWN TREASURES

The Royal Mile. It's a name that conjures images of history, of kings and queens, of ancient stones and whispered secrets. But for me, it started with a map, a faded, hand-drawn thing my grandfather had left behind. It wasn't a tourist map, all neat lines and labeled attractions. This one was different. It had strange symbols, cryptic notes, and a single phrase scrawled in the corner: "Where shadows lengthen, secrets awaken." He'd always been fascinated by Edinburgh's Old Town, by the way the past seemed to seep from its very stones. He said the Royal Mile wasn't just a street; it was a living history, a place where time itself seemed to bend.

That's how I found myself standing at the top of the Mile, the castle looming behind me, the city stretching out below. It felt like stepping into a story, a story I was only just beginning to understand. The air was thick with the scent of old stone and damp earth, and the sound of bagpipes drifted from a nearby close, a haunting melody that seemed to echo through the centuries. This chapter isn't just about walking a famous street. It's about unlocking the secrets hidden in its shadows, about feeling the pulse of history beneath your feet. It's about understanding that the Royal Mile isn't just a tourist attraction; it's a living, breathing testament to Edinburgh's past.

Let's start at the top, at the castle. It's more than just a fortress; it's a symbol of Scotland itself, a place where kings were crowned and battles were fought. Walking its ramparts, you can almost hear the clash of swords and the roar of cannons. The views from up there are breathtaking, but don't just snap a photo and move on. Take a moment to feel the weight of history, to imagine the lives that have been lived within those walls.

Now, down the Mile we go. But don't just stick to the main street. Venture into the closes and wynds, the narrow alleyways that branch off like hidden veins. These are the places where the real Edinburgh lies, the places where the shadows lengthen and the secrets awaken. Each close has a story to tell, a tale of merchants and murderers, of poets and paupers.

Take Mary King's Close, for example. It's a preserved street, buried beneath the modern city, a snapshot of life in 17th-century Edinburgh. Walking its cobbled stones, you can

this was a separate burgh.

But the Royal Mile isn't just about the past. It's also about the present. It's a place where tourists mingle with locals, where street performers entertain crowds, where shops sell everything from tartan scarves to whisky miniatures. It's a vibrant, bustling place, a microcosm of Edinburgh itself.

And speaking of whisky, don't miss the Scotch Whisky Experience. It's a bit touristy, but it's a great way to learn about Scotland's national drink. You can even take a tasting tour and sample some of the finest malts.

But the real magic of the Royal Mile lies in its atmosphere. It's the way the light filters through

almost hear the voices of the people who lived and died there, the whispers of plague victims and the cries of street vendors.

And then there's the Canongate, the lower part of the Mile. It's quieter, more residential, but it's just as rich in history. Look for the hidden courtyards, the ancient churches, the remnants of a time when

the ancient buildings, the way the wind whispers through the closes, the way the history seems to hang in the air like a mist. It's a place that gets under your skin, that makes you feel like you've stepped into a different world.

Here's a tip: walk the Mile at night. When the crowds have thinned and the streetlights cast long shadows, the place takes on a different character. It becomes more mysterious, more atmospheric, more like the Edinburgh of my grandfather's stories.

And as you walk, keep your eyes open for the strange symbols on my grandfather's map.

He said they were clues, markers of places where the veil between worlds was thin. I don't know what they mean, but I have a feeling they're important.

This isn't just a sightseeing trip. It's a journey into the heart of Edinburgh's history, a quest to uncover the secrets that lie hidden in its shadows. And who knows? Maybe, just maybe, you'll find a piece of your own story along the way.

Remember that Edinburgh is a city of stories. The Royal Mile is its spine, its central thread, connecting the past and the present. Take the time to listen to the whispers of the stones, to feel the pulse of history beneath your feet. Let the stories seep into your soul, and you'll find that the Royal Mile isn't just a street; it's a portal to another time.

And as you explore, consider this: what are you looking for? What draws you to the Royal Mile? Is it the history, the architecture, the atmosphere? Or is it something more, something you can't quite put into words? Whatever it is, embrace it. Let it guide you. And be prepared to be surprised. Because the Royal Mile has a way of revealing its secrets to those who are willing to look. This is more than a walk. It's an exploration. And as you step onto the cobbled stones and begin your journey, remember that you're not just a tourist; you're a traveler, an explorer, a seeker. And who knows what you might find?

Let's walk the Royal Mile, not as a tourist, but as someone who wants to understand the heartbeat of Edinburgh. The stones beneath your feet, they aren't just paving. They're a timeline, a record of centuries. Think about it: Mary Queen of Scots walked these very stones. John Knox preached fire and brimstone. Robert Louis Stevenson found inspiration in these alleyways. This isn't just a street; it's a living, breathing history book, and you're walking through its pages.

Start at the top, at the castle esplanade. The sheer weight of history here is palpable. From this vantage point, you see the city spread out, but you also feel the strategic importance of this place. It's easy to understand why generations fought and died for this rock. The castle itself is a maze of stories. Each

Remember that Edinburgh is a city of stories. The Royal Mile is its spine, its central thread, connecting the past and the present. Take the time to listen to the whispers of the stones, to feel the pulse of history beneath your feet. Let the stories seep into your soul, and you'll find that the Royal Mile isn't just a street; it's a portal to another time.

And as you explore, consider this: what are you looking for? What draws you to the Royal Mile? Is it the history, the architecture, the atmosphere? Or is it something more, something you can't quite put into words? Whatever it is, embrace it. Let it guide you. And be prepared to be surprised. Because the Royal Mile has a way of revealing its secrets to those who are willing to look. This is more than a walk. It's an exploration. And as you step onto the cobbled stones and begin your journey, remember that you're not just a tourist; you're a traveler, an explorer, a seeker. And who knows what you might find?

Let's walk the Royal Mile, not as a tourist, but as someone who wants to understand the heartbeat of Edinburgh. The stones beneath your feet, they aren't just paving. They're a timeline, a record of centuries. Think about it: Mary Queen of Scots walked these very stones. John Knox preached fire and brimstone. Robert Louis Stevenson found inspiration in these alleyways. This isn't just a street; it's a living, breathing history book, and you're walking through its pages.

Start at the top, at the castle esplanade. The sheer weight of history here is palpable. From this vantage point, you see the city spread out, but you also feel the strategic importance of this place. It's easy to understand why generations fought and died for this rock. The castle itself is a maze of stories. Each

- Walk the ramparts and take inthe panoramic views of the city.

The Royal Mile, the closes, the castle – they're all part of a larger story, a story that's still being written. And you, as a visitor, are part of that story. You're not just observing the past; you're experiencing it, feeling it, becoming a part of it.

Remember, this isn't just about seeing the sights; it's about understanding them. It's about feeling the weight of history, the pulse of the city. It's about connecting with the past and the present, about realizing that you're walking in the footsteps of kings and commoners, poets and paupers.

And as you explore, keep your senses open. Listen to the whispers of the stones, feel the wind on your face, smell the damp earth. Let the city speak to you, let it tell you its stories.

When you get to the cities, here's how to think about it: You're not just going to a place; you're experiencing it.

Let's say you are ready to venture from Edinburgh to Glasgow. To get there, you have a few options, but the train is by far the most efficient and enjoyable. Trains depart regularly from Edinburgh Waverley, and the journey takes about an hour. Once you arrive at Glasgow Central, you'll find yourself in the heart of the city.

Glasgow has a different energy from Edinburgh. It's grittier, more industrial, but also incredibly vibrant and creative.

- Explore the Kelvingrove Art Gallery and Museum, a treasure trove of art and artifacts.
- Wander through the Merchant City, a stylish district filled with shops, restaurants, and bars.
- Check out the street art scene, which is one of the best in Europe.

For places to stay, Glasgow offers a range of options, from budget-friendly hostels to luxurious hotels. If you want to be in the center of the action, look for accommodation near the city center.

Food and drink in Glasgow are a delight. The city has a thriving culinary scene, with everything from traditional Scottish fare to international cuisine.

- Try a Glasgow curry, a local specialty.
- Sample some of the local craft beers.
- Visit a traditional pub for a dram of whisky.

When you are ready to explore Inverness from Edinburgh, you have the option of taking a train or bus, but if you want to really experience the

Highlands, I recommend renting a car. This will give you the freedom to explore at your own pace.

Inverness is the gateway to the Highlands, and there's so much to see and do.

- Visit Loch Ness, home to the legendary Nessie.
- Explore the Cairngorms National Park, a vast wilderness of mountains and forests.
- Take a boat trip on the Moray Firth, where you can see dolphins and seals.

Accommodation in Inverness ranges from cozy bed and breakfasts to grand hotels. For food, try some of the local seafood or game. And don't forget to sample some of the Highland whiskies.

Traveling to Aberdeen from Edinburgh is also best done by train or car. Aberdeen, the Granite City, has a unique character, shaped by its maritime history and oil industry

- Visit the Maritime Museum, which tells the story of Aberdeen's seafaring past.
- Explore Old Aberdeen, a historic district with cobbled streets and ancient buildings.
- Take a walk along the beach, which stretches for miles along the coast.

Aberdeen has a good selection of hotels and restaurants. For food, try some of the fresh seafood or the local beef. And, of course, there are plenty of pubs where you can try some of the local beers.

Remember, travel is about more than just seeing places. It's about experiencing them, feeling them, connecting with them. So, as you explore Scotland, keep your senses open, your mind curious, and your heart receptive. You never know what you might discover.

WHISKY TOURS

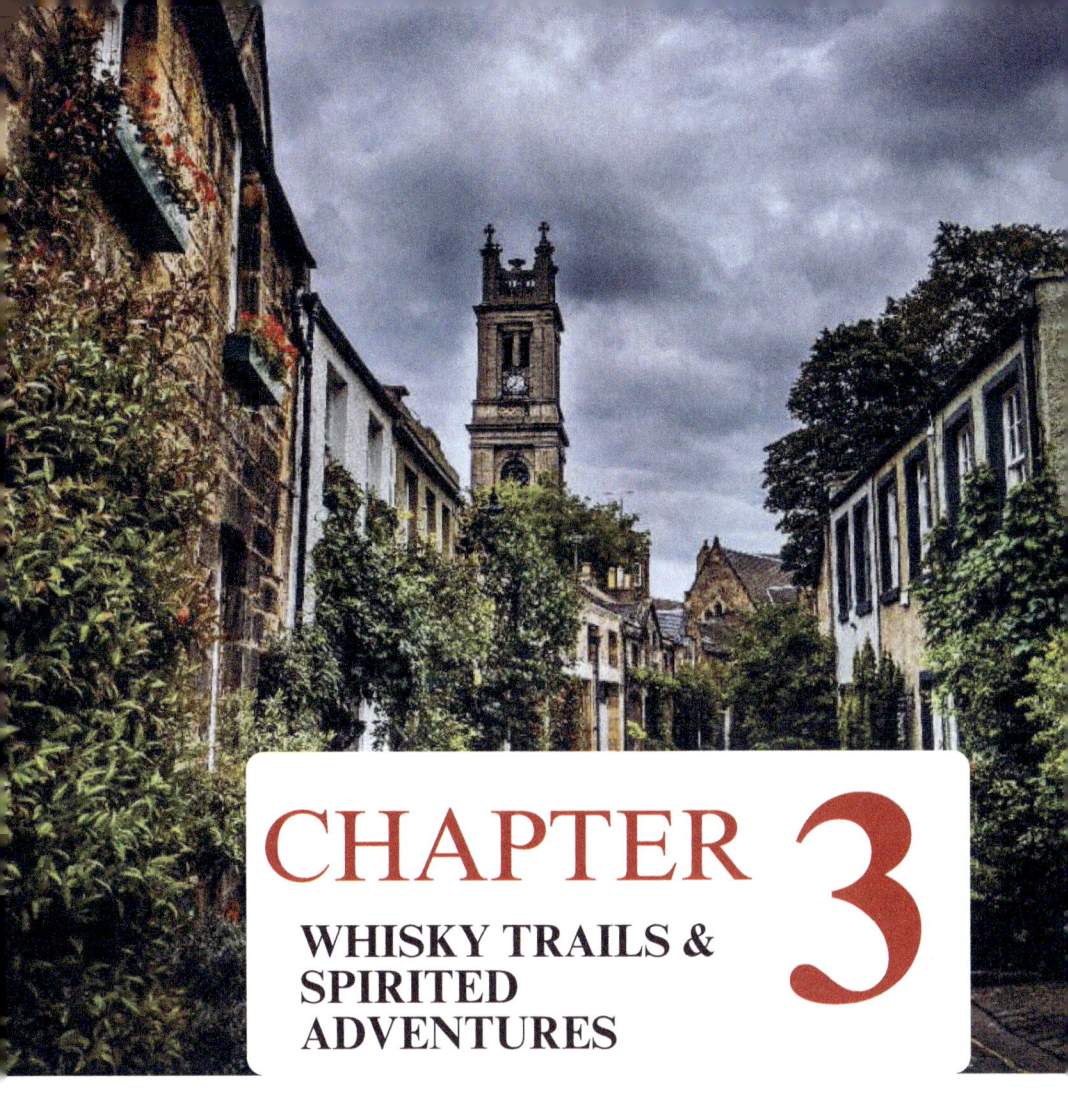

CHAPTER 3
WHISKY TRAILS & SPIRITED ADVENTURES

This chapter is more than a guide to whisky tours. It's an exploration of a tradition, a journey into the heart of a culture that's as rich and complex as the spirit itself. It's about feeling the passion that goes into every barrel, about understanding that whisky isn't just a drink; it's a living, breathing part of Scotland's heritage.

Let's start with the basics. Whisky is made from barley, water, and yeast. But it's the way these ingredients are combined,the way they're nurtured, that makes Scottish whisky so unique.

The peat smoke, the pure spring water, the sea air – they all contribute to the distinct flavors that vary from region to region.

The Highlands, for example, produce whiskies that are often smoky and robust, with notes of heather and spice. The Speyside region, on the other hand, is known for its sweet and fruity whiskies, with hints of honey and vanilla. The islands, like Islay and Skye, produce whiskies that are intensely peaty and maritime, with notes of seaweed and salt.

But whisky isn't just about the taste. It's about the experience. It's about visiting the distilleries, walking through the warehouses, and talking to the people who make it. These are the places where the stories are told, where the traditions are kept alive.

Take a tour of a distillery, and you'll learn about the process, from malting to distilling to aging. You'll see the copper stills, the oak barrels, the warehouses where the whisky slowly matures. You'll hear the stories of the distillers, their passion, their dedication, their connection to the land.

- Visit a distillery in Speyside for a sweet and fruity experience.
- Explore Islay for a peaty and smoky adventure.
- Try a tasting tour to learn about the different whisky regions.

But don't just stick to the big-name distilleries. Venture off the beaten path, and you'll find hidden gems, small family-run distilleries that have been making whisky for generations. These are the places where you'll find the real spirit of

Scotland.

And speaking of spirits, don't forget the pubs. They're an integral part of Scottish whisky culture. These are the places where locals gather to share stories, to celebrate, to mourn. They're the places where you can experience the true warmth and hospitality of the Scottish people.

Order a dram of your favorite whisky, and you'll likely find yourself drawn into a conversation. You'll hear tales of smugglers and distillers, of ghosts and faeries, of the legends that surround this iconic drink.

- Find a traditional pub with a good selection of whiskies.
- Ask the bartender for recommendations.
- Try a whisky flight to sample different malts.

But whisky isn't just about drinking. It's about appreciating the craft, the history, the culture. It's about understanding that every bottle tells a story, a story that's been passed down through generations.

And as you explore, keep your senses open. Smell the peat smoke, taste the different flavors, listen to the stories. Let the whisky take you on a journey, a journey into the heart of Scotland.

Remember, this isn't just about drinking whisky. It's about experiencing it. It's about feeling the passion, the history, the tradition. It's about connecting with the soul of Scotland.

And as you explore, consider this: what are you looking for? What draws you to Scottish whisky? Is it the taste, the history, the culture? Or is it something more,

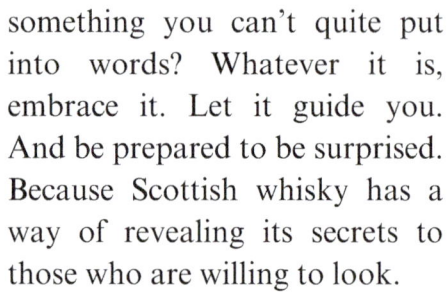

something you can't quite put into words? Whatever it is, embrace it. Let it guide you. And be prepared to be surprised. Because Scottish whisky has a way of revealing its secrets to those who are willing to look.

This is more than a tour. It's an exploration. And as you raise your glass and take your first sip, remember that you're not just drinking whisky; you're tasting history, you're experiencing a tradition, you're connecting with the spirit of Scotland.

Let's talk whisky. Not just as a drink, but as an art, a science, a cultural touchstone. A visit to a Scottish distillery is more than a tour; it's an immersion. You're stepping into a world where time slows down,

where tradition reigns, and where every drop tells a story. The process itself is fascinating. Barley, water, yeast – simple ingredients transformed through skill and patience into something extraordinary. You'll see the mash tuns, the copper pot stills, the oak casks where the spirit matures, each stage carefully monitored by experienced hands.

Each distillery has its own character, its own secrets. The location, the water source, the shape of the stills, the type of oak used for aging – all these factors contribute to the unique flavor of the whisky. A tour is a chance to understand this alchemy, to appreciate the craftsmanship that goes into every bottle. And of course, there's the tasting. This isn't just about drinking; it's about savoring. You'll learn how to nose the whisky, to identify the different aromas, to understand the complex layers of flavor.

- Take a tour of a distillery in the Speyside region to experience the sweeter, fruitier whiskies.
- Visit a distillery on Islay for a taste of the peaty, smoky malts.
- Consider a tasting experience that pairs whisky with local foods.

But whisky is more than just a drink. It's woven into the fabric of Scottish culture. It's part of celebrations, of rituals, of everyday life. It's a symbol of hospitality, of warmth, of shared experience. You'll find it in pubs, in homes, in gatherings of friends and family. It's a way of connecting, of sharing stories, of celebrating life.

The language of whisky is rich with tradition. You'll hear terms like "dram," "cask strength," "single malt," each with its own meaning, its own history. And you'll learn that whisky isn't just about the taste; it's about the story behind it, the place it came from, the people who made it.

And then there are the pubs. They're the heart of Scottish social life, the places where locals gather to unwind, to chat, to listen to music. You'll find pubs of all kinds, from traditional establishments with roaring fireplaces and dark wood paneling to modern bars with craft beers and whisky cocktails.

But the real magic of a Scottish pub is the atmosphere. It's the sound of laughter, the clinking of glasses, the warmth of the conversation. It's the feeling of being part of a community, of sharing a moment with strangers who quickly become friends. And of course, there's the whisky. You'll find a wide selection, from well-known brands to local distilleries, each with its own unique flavor.

- Seek out traditional pubs in small towns for an authentic experience.
- Try a local beer or a traditional Scottish ale.
- Explore the restaurants in the city center for a range of dining options.

Remember, this isn't just about drinking. It's about experiencing the culture, the history, the tradition. It's about connecting with the soul of Scotland. And as you raise your glass and take your first sip, remember that you're not just drinking whisky; you're tasting history, you're experiencing a tradition, you're connecting with the spirit of Scotland.

KINLOCHLEVEN

CHAPTER 4
HIGHLAND & LOWLAND ESCAPES

The wind howled a mournful tune, a constant, low drone that vibrated through the old bones of the Land Rover. Rain, not the gentle drizzle Edinburgh knew, but a proper, horizontal deluge, hammered against the windscreen. I was lost. Not geographically, not entirely. The GPS, bless its digital heart, showed a thin line snaking through the Highlands, a road barely more than a sheep track. But I was lost in that deeper sense, the one where the landscape swallows you whole, and you feel a million miles from everything familiar.

It started with a faded photograph, tucked into a second-hand bookshop on Victoria Street. A black and white image of a lone cottage, perched on the edge of a loch, surrounded by mountains that seemed to pierce the sky. On the back, a single word: "Kinlochleven." No directions, no coordinates, just a name, a whisper.

Something about that image, the stark beauty, the sense of isolation, resonated deep within me. I'd spent days exploring Edinburgh's cobbled streets, its historic closes, its vibrant pubs. But the city, for all its charm, felt like a prelude, a taste of something greater. I yearned for the wild heart of Scotland, the raw, untamed landscapes that whispered of ancient secrets.

So, I set off, following the faded photograph as my compass. The road narrowed, the tarmac giving way to gravel, then to rough, uneven tracks. The landscape shifted, from rolling hills to towering mountains, from lush green valleys to stark, windswept moors. The air grew colder, the scent of heather and peat filling my lungs.

Kinlochleven, when I finally found it, was a scattering of stone cottages, huddled together against the elements. The loch, dark and brooding, reflected the mountains like a mirror, the water rippling with the force of the wind. The cottage from the photograph, its roof moss-covered, its windows dark, stood silent, a sentinel on the edge of the world.

I parked the Land Rover, the engine sighing as it fell silent, and stepped out into the rain. The wind whipped at my coat, the rain stinging my face. I walked towards the cottage, drawn by an unseen force, a sense of something ancient and powerful.

The door creaked open, revealing a dark, musty interior. The air was thick with the scent of damp wood and peat smoke. A fire burned in the hearth, casting flickering shadows across the stone walls. An old woman sat by the fire, her face etched with the lines of time, her eyes as deep and dark as the loch.

She didn't speak, but simply gestured for me to sit. I sat, the silence broken only by the crackling of the fire and the howling of the wind. She poured me a dram of whisky, its peaty aroma filling the air. It burned my throat, but warmed me from the inside out.

Then, she began to speak, her voice low and melodic, the words a mix of English and Gaelic. She told me stories of the mountains, of the ancient spirits that dwelled within them, of the hidden glens where the fairies danced on moonlit nights. She spoke of the loch, of the kelpies that lurked beneath its surface, of the secrets it held within its depths.

She told me of the history of Kinlochleven, of the lost village of Glencoe,and the massacre that occurred there.

Her voice echoed with the weight of generations, with the pain and the beauty of the land.

As the night wore on, the stories grew stranger, more mystical. She spoke of standing stones that pulsed with ancient energy, of hidden caves where the old gods still whispered, of the northern lights that danced across the sky like spirits.

She told me that the land remembers, that the mountains hold the echoes of the past, that the lochs whisper secrets to those who listen. She told me that Scotland is a land of magic, a place where the veil between worlds is thin.

I left Kinlochleven as the first rays of dawn painted the sky, the rain finally ceasing. The old woman stood at the door of the cottage, her silhouette framed against the rising sun. She didn't wave, but simply watched as I drove away, the image of her etched into my memory.

The journey back was a blur, the landscape passing by in a dreamlike haze. I felt changed, transformed by the stories, by the magic of the land. I had glimpsed a world beyond the ordinary, a world where the ancient spirits still roamed, where the mountains held secrets, and the lochs whispered tales.

This experience, this feeling, is what I want to share with you. To venture past the well-trodden paths of Edinburgh, to explore the Highlands and Lowlands, is to discover the true heart of Scotland.

- The Lowlands' Gentle Beauty: Don't underestimate the Lowlands. Places like the Scottish Borders are full of abbeys and castles. The rolling hills and quiet valleys are a perfect counterpoint to the dramatic Highlands. Visit places such as Dryburgh Abbey, or take a walk along the River Tweed.
- The Highlands' Rugged Majesty: The Highlands are a world unto themselves. Loch Ness, with its mysterious depths, is a must-see. Drive

through Glencoe, its dramatic peaks and deep valleys a testament to the power of nature. Explore the Isle of Skye, with its jagged mountains and crystal-clear pools.

- The Islands' Wild Spirit: The Outer Hebrides, the Orkney Islands, the Shetland Islands – each has its own unique character. The wind-swept beaches, the ancient standing stones, the vibrant island cultures – they will leave you breathless. The Orkney Islands, for example, are home to Skara Brae, a Neolithic village preserved in time.

- Whisky and Culture: The Speyside region is the heart of Scotch whisky country. Visit distilleries, learn about the art of whisky making, and sample some of the finest drams in the world. And don't forget the vibrant music scene, the traditional ceilidhs, the storytelling sessions – they are all part of the Scottish experience.
- Practical Highland Tips: Be prepared for unpredictable weather. Pack

layers, waterproofs, and sturdy boots. Driving can be challenging, with narrow roads and winding passes. Allow plenty of time for travel, and be prepared for delays. Midges can be a nuisance in the summer, so pack insect repellent. Respect the land, and leave no trace.
- Local Interactions: The people of the Highlands and Islands are known for their warmth and hospitality. Take the time to talk to locals, to learn about their stories, their traditions, their way of life. You may find that the most memorable experiences are the ones you least expect.

Scotland is a land of contrasts, a place where the ancient and the modern coexist, where the wild and the gentle intertwine. It is a land that will capture your heart, that will stir your soul, that will leave you forever changed.

The mists curl around Loch Ness, a dark, liquid mystery reflecting the craggy peaks that surround it. Here, the air itself hums with possibility, the very water seems to hold its breath, waiting. You don't just visit Loch Ness; you enter a realm of legend. The drive along its shores, whether from Inverness or Fort William, is a journey into a landscape carved by glaciers and time. The dark, peat-stained waters, stretching for over 20 miles, invite you to scan their depths, your eyes searching for the elusive Nessie. You can take a boat trip, of course, the sonar pinging, the guide narrating tales of sightings and scientific investigations, but the real experience is in the quiet moments, standing on the shore, the wind whipping at your hair, the silence broken only by the cry of a distant bird.

The Highlands, in general, are a masterclass in raw, unadulterated beauty. The sheer scale of the mountains, the deep, verdant glens, the rushing waterfalls – it's a landscape that demands your attention. Driving here, you'll find yourself constantly pulling over, camera in hand, trying to capture the immensity of it all. You might find yourself in Glen Coe, its dramatic peaks a stark reminder of the area's tragic history, or you could explore the Cairngorms, a vast wilderness of forests, lochs, and mountains. The trails here are endless, offering hikes for every level, from gentle strolls to challenging climbs.

Leaving the dramatic Highlands, we descend into the Lowlands, where the landscape shifts from rugged peaks to rolling hills, and the air is filled with the echoes of ancient battles and royal intrigue. Stirling, a city steeped in history, stands as a testament to Scotland's turbulent past. Stirling Castle, perched atop a volcanic crag, dominates the skyline, its walls whispering tales of kings and queens, of sieges and triumphs. Walking its ramparts, you can almost hear the clash of swords, the roar of battle. The views from the castle are breathtaking, stretching across the Forth Valley, a patchwork of fields and forests.

The Lowlands offer a different kind of beauty, a gentler, more pastoral landscape. You can explore the ruins of ancient abbeys, wander through charming villages, and discover hidden gems tucked away in the countryside. The area around Stirling is rich with historical sites, from the Bannockburn

battlefield, where Robert the Bruce led the Scots to victory, to the Wallace Monument, a towering tribute to Scotland's national hero.

Venturing beyond the main cities, day trips offer a glimpse into Scotland's coastal charms and historic towns. From Edinburgh, a short train ride will take you to North Berwick, a charming seaside town with golden beaches and stunning views of the Bass Rock, a volcanic island teeming with seabirds.

You can explore the ruins of Tantallon Castle, perched on a cliff overlooking the sea, or take a boat trip to the Isle of May, a nature reserve home to puffins and seals.

- Getting to North Berwick from Edinburgh: Regular train services operate from Edinburgh Waverley station, taking approximately 30 minutes.
- Things to do: Explore the beaches, visit the Scottish Seabird Centre, explore Tantallon Castle, take a boat trip to the Isle of May, play golf at one of the championship courses.
- Where to stay: North Berwick offers a range of accommodation options, from hotels and guest houses to self-catering cottages.
- Food and beverages: Enjoy fresh seafood at local restaurants, try traditional fish and chips, and sample local beers and whiskies.

Another excellent day trip option is St Andrews, the home of golf and Scotland's oldest university. The town is a mix of medieval charm and modern vibrancy, with historic buildings, bustling shops, and a lively student population. You can walk along the iconic Old Course, visit the ruins of St Andrews Cathedral, or explore the university campus.

- Getting to St Andrews from Edinburgh: Regular bus services operate from Edinburgh bus station, taking approximately 1 hour and 30 minutes.
- Things to do: Walk the Old Course, visit St Andrews Cathedral and Castle, explore the University of St Andrews, relax on the beaches, visit the British Golf Museum.
- Where to stay: St Andrews offers a range of accommodation options, from luxury hotels to budget-friendly guest houses.
- Food and beverages: Enjoy fine dining at Michelin-starred restaurants, try traditional Scottish fare at local pubs, and sample local whiskies and craft beers.

For a taste of Scotland's fishing heritage, visit the picturesque town of Anstruther, in the East Neuk of Fife. Here, you can watch the fishing boats returning to harbor, sample fresh seafood at the local fish and chip shops, and explore the charming harbor area.

- Getting to **Anstruther** from Edinburgh: Regular bus services operate from Edinburgh bus station, with changes required, taking approximately 2 hours.
- Things to do: Explore the harbor, visit the Scottish Fisheries Museum, walk along the Fife Coastal Path, enjoy fresh seafood.

- Where to stay: Anstruther offers a range of accommodation options, from guest houses and bed and breakfasts to self-catering cottages.
- Food and beverages: Enjoy fresh seafood, particularly fish and chips, at local restaurants.

These day trips offer a chance to explore the diverse landscapes and rich history of Scotland, all within easy reach of Edinburgh. Each town offers a unique experience, a glimpse into a different aspect of Scottish life.

Scotland is a land of contrasts, a place where ancient history meets modern vibrancy, where rugged landscapes meet charming towns. It's a land that will capture your imagination, stir your soul, and leave you with memories that will last a lifetime.

BAUTA

CHAPTER 5
A TASTE OF SCOTLAND

The scent hit me first, a smoky, earthy aroma that clung to the air like a whispered secret. It wasn't the clean, crisp scent of a distillery, nor the sharp tang of the sea. This was something deeper, something primal. I'd been chasing a rumour, a whisper of a hidden bothy deep in the Cairngorms, where a reclusive old woman brewed a broth that, they said, held the very essence of Scotland. Not a fancy restaurant, not a tourist trap, but something raw, authentic.

I'd spent days navigating winding roads, following hand-drawn maps and cryptic directions from locals who spoke in hushed tones, their eyes gleaming with a mix of reverence and apprehension. The path, if you could call it that, had narrowed to a barely visible track, swallowed by heather and the encroaching shadows of the mountains. The air grew colder, the silence broken only by the crunch of my boots on the rough terrain and the distant cry of a buzzard.

The bothy, when I finally found it, was a low, stone structure, its roof barely distinguishable from the surrounding rocks. Smoke curled from a chimney, a thin, grey ribbon against the darkening sky. The door, a rough-hewn slab of wood, creaked open as I approached, revealing a dimly lit interior.

Inside, the old woman sat by a crackling fire, her face etched with the lines of time, her eyes as bright and sharp as a winter's day. A large iron pot bubbled over the flames, the smoky aroma filling the small space. She didn't speak, but gestured for me to sit, her movements slow and deliberate.

She ladled a steaming bowl of broth, the liquid dark and thick, flecked with herbs and spices I couldn't identify. The first sip was a revelation, a symphony of flavors that exploded on my tongue. It was earthy and smoky, sweet and savory, with a hint of something wild and untamed. It was a taste of the land itself, of the heather-clad hills, the peat-rich soil, the windswept moors.

As I ate, she began to speak, her voice low and melodic, the words a mix of English and Gaelic. She spoke of the ancient ways, of the connection between the land and its people, of the power of food to nourish both body and soul. She told me the

stories behind the ingredients, each herb and spice carefully chosen for its medicinal and spiritual properties.

She explained the importance of seasonal eating, of using what the land provided, of respecting the cycles of nature. She spoke of the wild game that roamed the mountains, of the fish that swam in the lochs, of the berries that grew in the glens.

This wasn't just a meal; it was an experience, a journey into the heart of Scottish culinary tradition. It was a taste of Scotland, not the tourist-friendly version, but the real, authentic taste, the taste of the land, the taste of history, the taste of magic.

This is the Scotland I want you to experience, a Scotland where food is more than just sustenance, it's a story, a connection to the past, a celebration of the present.

- **The Hearty Comfort of Scottish Cuisine:** Forget the bland stereotypes. Scottish food is a rich and diverse tapestry of flavors, from hearty stews and game pies to fresh seafood and artisan cheeses. Seek

out the local pubs, the farm-to-table restaurants, the hidden cafes where the food is made with passion and pride.
- **The "Water of Life"**: Whisky's Deep Roots: Whisky is more than just a drink; it's a cultural icon, a symbol of Scottish hospitality and craftsmanship. Explore the distilleries of Speyside, Islay, and the Highlands, where you can learn about the art of whisky making and sample a dram or two. Be mindful to drink responsibly, and learn the subtle nuances of each regions product.
- **Seafood Sensations**: Scotland's coast is a treasure trove of seafood delights, from plump scallops and succulent langoustines to flaky haddock and creamy mussels. Venture to the fishing villages of the East Neuk of Fife or the Isle of Skye, where you can savor the freshest catches of the day.
- **The Art of Baking**: From buttery shortbread and flaky oatcakes to rich fruitcakes and sticky toffee pudding, Scottish baking is a testament to the country's love of sweet treats. Visit local bakeries and tea rooms, where you can indulge in these delectable delights.
- **Modern Scottish Cuisine:** A new generation of chefs is reinventing Scottish cuisine, blending traditional ingredients with innovative techniques. Explore the vibrant food scenes of Edinburgh and Glasgow, where you can find Michelin-starred restaurants and trendy bistros serving up contemporary Scottish fare.
- **The Importance of Local Produce**: Scotland's fertile lands and pristine waters produce a bounty of high-quality ingredients, from Aberdeen Angus beef and wild venison to seasonal fruits and vegetables. Seek out farmers' markets and local producers, where you can sample the freshest and most flavorful ingredients.
- The Social Aspect of Food: Food is an integral part of

Scottish social life, a way to connect with friends and family, to celebrate traditions, and to share stories. Join a ceilidh, a traditional Scottish gathering with music and dancing, where you can enjoy hearty food and lively conversation.

Scotland's culinary landscape is a reflection of its diverse landscapes, its rich history, and its vibrant culture. It's a journey for the senses, a chance to taste the true essence of this remarkable land.

Edinburgh's culinary landscape is a delightful paradox, a place where tradition and innovation dance a spirited reel. Forget any preconceived notions of stodgy fare; this city pulses with a vibrant foodie scene that caters to every palate, from the intrepid adventurer seeking the authentic taste of haggis to the discerning gourmand in pursuit of Michelin-starred artistry. The city's historical heart, with its cobblestone closes and hidden courtyards, holds within it a wealth of modern gastronomic treasures.

Let's begin with the iconic haggis. Yes, it's a dish that often elicits raised eyebrows, but to truly experience Scotland, you must embrace it. Seek out a local pub, a place where the haggis is prepared with pride, the recipe passed down through generations. You'll find it's a surprisingly complex dish, a savory blend of oatmeal, spices, and sheep's offal, served with neeps and tatties (mashed turnips and potatoes). It's a hearty, warming meal, perfect for a chilly Edinburgh evening.

But Edinburgh's culinary scene extends far beyond traditional fare. A new generation of chefs is transforming the city's dining landscape, infusing Scottish ingredients with global influences, creating innovative dishes that are both exciting and delicious. You'll find restaurants showcasing seasonal produce, highlighting the bounty of Scotland's larder, from wild game and fresh seafood to artisan cheeses and craft beers.

Venturing beyond Edinburgh, you'll discover the regional specialties that define Scotland's diverse culinary identity. The coastal towns, from the East Neuk of Fife to the Isle of Skye, offer a seafood lover's paradise. You'll find plump scallops, succulent langoustines, and flaky haddock, all caught fresh from the surrounding waters. Inland, the rolling hills and rugged mountains provide a habitat for wild game, including venison, grouse, and pheasant
.

Scotland's larder is also rich in local produce, from the berries that grow wild in the glens to the artisan cheeses produced on small farms. Seek out farmers' markets and local producers, where you can sample the freshest and most flavorful ingredients. The quality of Scottish beef and lamb is also world renowned, and a must try for meat lovers.

To truly immerse yourself in Edinburgh's foodie scene, you must explore its culinary hotspots. The city is home to a wealth of restaurants, from Michelin-starred establishments to cozy bistros, each offering a unique dining experience. You'll find trendy bars serving up craft cocktails, and traditional pubs pouring local beers and whiskies.

- **Getting around Edinburgh:** Edinburgh is a very walkable city, however, it also has excellent bus and tram services. Taxis and ride-sharing are also readily available.
- **Where to stay in Edinburgh:** Edinburgh offers a wide range of accommodation options, from luxury hotels and boutique guesthouses to budget-friendly hostels and apartments.
- **Food and Beverages**: Beyond Haggis, Edinburgh has a thriving food scene. From Michelin star restaurants to street food. The city also offers a wide range of local beers, gins, and of course, Scotch Whisky.

The city's markets are also a must-visit for any foodie. The Edinburgh Farmers' Market, held every Saturday, is a vibrant showcase of local produce, artisan cheeses, and baked goods. The Grassmarket area offers a collection of pubs and restaurants with outside seating, and is a great area for people watching.

For a truly immersive culinary experience, consider taking a food tour. Several companies offer guided tours of Edinburgh's food scene, taking you to hidden gems and local favorites. You can also take a whisky tasting tour, learning about the art of whisky making and sampling a few drams.

Beyond Edinburgh, consider a trip to Glasgow, Scotland's second-largest city. Glasgow's culinary scene is as vibrant and diverse as its population, offering a mix of traditional Scottish fare and international cuisine.

- **Getting to Glasgow from Edinburgh**: Regular train services operate between Edinburgh Waverley and Glasgow Queen Street stations, taking approximately 50 minutes. Regular bus services are also available.

- Things to do in Glasgow: Explore the city's museums and art galleries, visit the Glasgow Cathedral, walk through the Botanic Gardens, and enjoy the vibrant nightlife.
- Where to stay in Glasgow: Glasgow offers a range of accommodation options, from luxury hotels and boutique guesthouses to budget-friendly hostels and apartments.
- Food and Beverages: Glasgow is known for its diverse culinary scene, with a wide range of restaurants serving everything from traditional Scottish fare to international cuisine. The city also has a thriving craft beer scene and a number of whisky bars.

Glasgow also offers a wide range of culinary experiences, from cooking classes to food markets. The Barras Market, held every weekend, is a vibrant mix of food stalls, vintage clothing, and antiques.

Scotland's culinary scene is a reflection of its diverse landscapes, its rich history, and its vibrant culture. It's a journey for the senses, a chance to taste the true essence of this remarkable land.

MUSEUMS

CHAPTER 6

MUSEUMS & HISTORICAL NARRATIVES

The silence in the room was thick, almost tangible, broken only by the soft click of my camera shutter. I'd stumbled upon it by accident, a small, unassuming museum tucked away in a quiet corner of a Highland village. No grand entrance, no throngs of tourists, just a simple sign that read, "The Lost Stories of Glen Affric." I'd been drawn in by the name, a whisper of a place I'd only seen in faded photographs, a place of ancient forests and hidden glens, a place where time seemed to stand still.

Inside, the light was dim, the air heavy with the scent of old paper and polished wood. The exhibits were simple, a collection of faded photographs, handwritten letters, and worn artifacts. But it was the stories they told, the voices that echoed from the past, that held me captive. There were tales of the last of the Caledonian Forest, of the wildcat that roamed its depths, of the people who lived in harmony with the land.

One exhibit, a small glass case, held a collection of hand-carved wooden tools, each piece worn smooth by years of use. A handwritten note beside them spoke of a woman, a healer, who lived in the glen, her knowledge of the forest's secrets passed down through generations. It spoke of her connection to the land, her understanding of its rhythms, her ability to heal with herbs and rituals.

Another exhibit displayed a series of black and white photographs, capturing the faces of the people who once called Glen Affric home. Their eyes, etched with the hardships of life in the Highlands, held a quiet strength, a connection to a past that seemed both distant and immediate. I felt a sense of loss, a longing for a time when life was simpler, more connected to the natural world.

The museum wasn't just a collection of artifacts; it was a portal, a window into a world that had vanished, a world that still whispered its secrets to those who were willing to listen. It was a reminder that history isn't just about kings and battles, but about the lives of ordinary people, about their struggles, their triumphs, their connection to the land. This experience, this sense of connection to the past, is what I want to share with you. Scotland is a land rich in history, a land where the echoes of the past can be heard in the stones of its castles, in

The whispers of its glens, in the stories told in its museums.

- **Edinburgh's Historical Heart**: The National Museum of Scotland is a treasure trove of artifacts, spanning Scotland's history from prehistoric times to the present day. Explore the exhibits on the Vikings, the Jacobites, and the Scottish Enlightenment. The Writers' Museum celebrates Scotland's literary giants, from Robert Burns to Sir Walter Scott.
- **Glasgow's Industrial Legacy:** The Riverside Museum, with its striking architecture, showcases Glasgow's rich maritime and industrial history. The People's Palace tells the story of Glasgow's working-class people, their struggles and their triumphs.
- **Highland Tales and Clan Histories:** The Highland Folk Museum in Newtonmore offers a glimpse into Highland life through the centuries. Explore the reconstructed crofts, the traditional blackhouses, and the living history exhibits. Many small local museums are found

throughout the highlands and islands, detailing local clan history and the impacts of the highland clearances.

- **Ancient Stones and Prehistoric Mysteries:** The Callanish Stones on the Isle of Lewis are a circle of standing stones older than Stonehenge, a place where the wind whispers secrets from the dawn of time. Skara Brae on the Orkney Islands is a remarkably preserved Neolithic village, offering a glimpse into life in the Stone Age.
- **The Power of Storytelling:** Scotland is a land of storytellers, where history is passed down through songs, poems, and tales. Seek out local storytelling sessions, where you can hear the legends and myths of the Highlands and Islands. The Scottish Storytelling Centre in Edinburgh offers regular events and workshops.
- **Beyond the Grand Museums:** Don't overlook the smaller, more intimate museums that dot the Scottish landscape. These hidden gems often hold the most compelling stories, the most personal connections to the past.
- **Understanding the Clearances:** The Highland Clearances were a dark chapter in Scottish history, a period of forced evictions that scattered Highland communities across the globe. Many museums, particularly in the Highlands, address this period, giving a sobering look into the nations past.

Scotland's museums and historical sites are more than just places to see artifacts; they are gateways to the past, places where you can connect with the people who shaped this land, where you can understand the forces that have shaped its history. They are places where stories come alive, where the past whispers its secrets to those who are willing to listen.

SCOTLAND

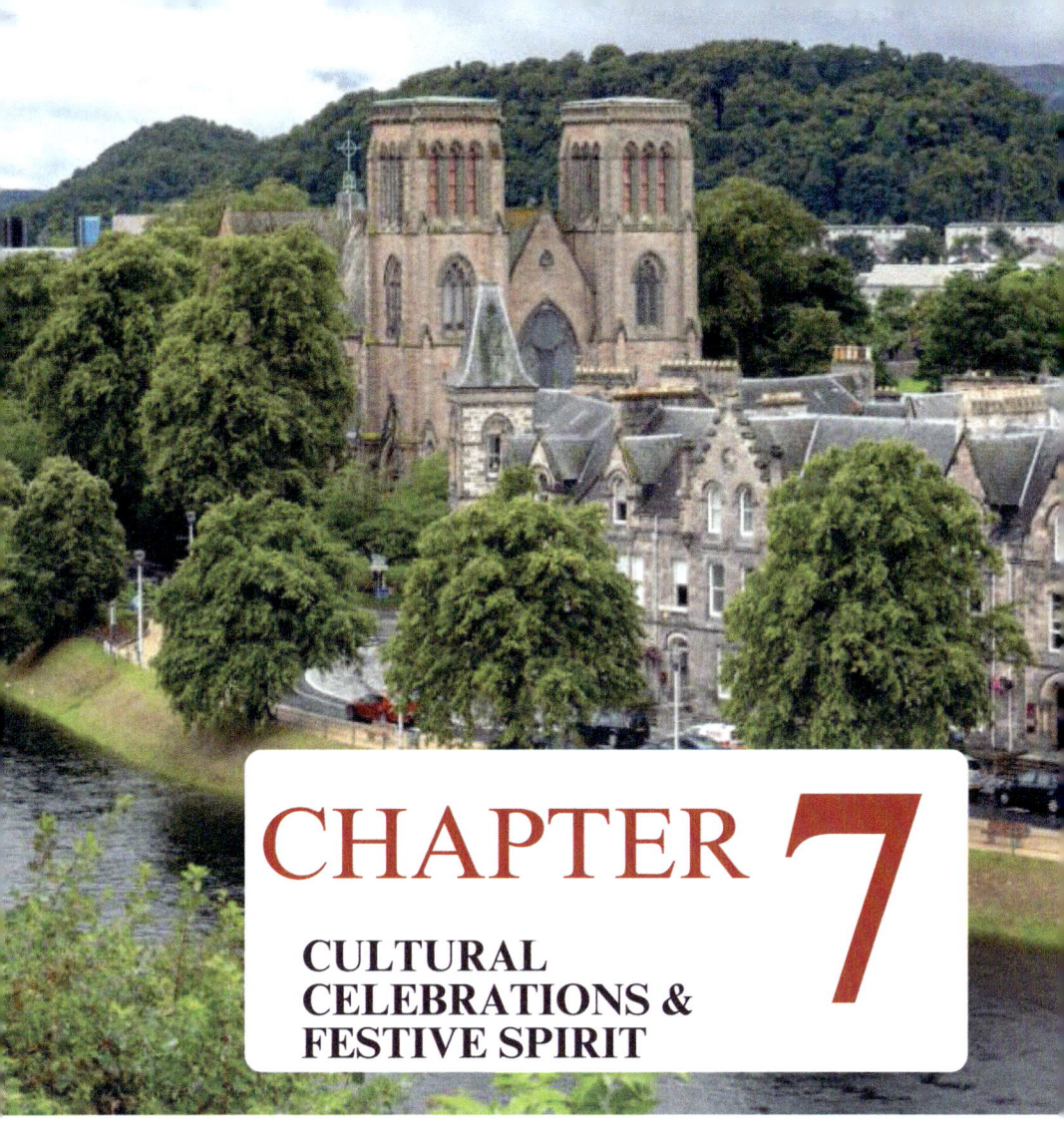

CHAPTER 7

CULTURAL CELEBRATIONS & FESTIVE SPIRIT

The drumming started low, a deep, rhythmic pulse that vibrated through the cobblestones, up through my boots, and into the very core of my being. It was late, well past midnight, and the biting wind whipped around the narrow streets of a small coastal town I'd stumbled upon. The sign outside, barely visible in the dim light, read "Stonehaven." I'd been drawn by the flickering glow of fire against the dark winter sky, a beacon in the vast, star-strewn expanse.

I followed the sound, the drumming growing louder, more insistent, until I emerged into a scene that felt like it belonged in a forgotten age. Figures, silhouetted against the flames, whirled and danced, their faces painted with soot and ash, their eyes gleaming with a wild, primal energy. They carried massive fireballs, swinging them in great arcs, the flames licking at the night sky. It was the Stonehaven Fireballs ceremony, a pagan ritual that predated recorded history, a celebration of the winter solstice, a defiant stand against the darkness.

I stood on the edge of the crowd, mesmerized, feeling a strange mix of awe and unease. The heat of the fire, the rhythmic drumming, the raw energy of the dancers – it was a sensory overload, a glimpse into a world where ancient traditions still held sway. I felt a connection to something deeper, something primal, a sense of belonging that transcended language and culture.

This experience, this immersion into the heart of a Scottish celebration, is what I want to share with you. Scotland is a land of festivals, a place where tradition and community come together in a vibrant display of cultural heritage. From the raucous revelry of Hogmanay to the ancient rituals of the Highland Games, Scotland's celebrations are a testament to the country's rich and diverse cultural tapestry.

- **Hogmanay: A Fiery New Year:** Forget the tame New Year's Eve celebrations you might be used to. Hogmanay in Scotland is a multi-day extravaganza, a whirlwind of music, dancing, and fire. Edinburgh's street party is legendary, with live bands, fireworks, and the traditional "first-footing." But don't overlook the smaller, more

intimate celebrations in towns and villages across the country, where the traditions are often more authentic.

- **Burns Night:** A Celebration of the Bard: On January 25th, Scotland celebrates the life and works of its national poet, Robert Burns. Expect hearty meals of haggis, neeps, and tatties, accompanied by recitations of Burns' poetry and lively ceilidh dancing. This is a night of warmth, camaraderie, and a healthy dose of Scottish pride.
- **Highland Games:** A Display of Strength and Tradition: The Highland Games are a summer staple, a celebration of Scottish athleticism and , heritage. Expect caber tossing, hammer throwing,and tug-of-war, along with pipe bands, Highland dancing, and traditional Scottish food and drink. Each region puts its own spin on the games, and many small towns hold their own competitions.
- Celtic Connections: A Musical Feast: Glasgow's Celtic Connections is a world-renowned festival of Celtic music, showcasing the best of traditional and contemporary artists from Scotland, Ireland, and beyond. Expect a diverse lineup of concerts, workshops, and ceilidhs.

- **Up Helly Aa**: A Viking Fire Festival: The Shetland Islands' Up Helly Aa is a spectacular fire festival, a tribute to the islands' Viking heritage. A torchlit procession culminates in the burning of a replica Viking longship, a sight that will leave you breathless. If you are going to visit the islands, do so during this festival.
- **The Fringe Festival:** Edinburgh transforms during the Fringe Festival. The world's largest arts festival. This is a time of pure creative energy. You can see shows of every type, and in every venue imaginable.
- **Local Festivals:** Each region of Scotland has its own unique festivals, celebrating local traditions and customs. Seek out these hidden gems, and you'll discover the true heart of Scottish culture.

Scotland's festivals are more than just entertainment; they are a window into the soul of the nation, a chance to connect with the people, the traditions, and the spirit of this remarkable land. They are a reminder that even in the modern world, ancient customs and cultural celebrations still hold a powerful sway, and that the festive spirit of Scotland is a thing to behold.

Edinburgh is a city that pulsates with creative energy, a place where festivals aren't just seasonal events, but a way of life. The city embraces celebration with an e

enthusiasm that transforms its historic streets into vibrant stages for artistic expression.From the world-renowned Edinburgh Festival Fringe, a sprawling celebration of theatre, comedy, and performance art, to the Edinburgh International Festival, a showcase of classical music, opera, and dance, the city offers a year-round calendar of cultural delights. The sheer scale of the Fringe, with its thousands of shows and countless venues, is a testament to the city's commitment to artistic freedom and innovation. You can wander through the Royal Mile, a living theatre where street performers compete for attention, or venture into hidden courtyards and underground venues, where experimental and avant-garde performances push the boundaries of artistic expression. The International Festival, by contrast, offers a more refined experience, showcasing world-class orchestras, renowned theatre companies, and celebrated opera singers.

Beyond the major festivals, Edinburgh hosts a diverse range of smaller events, each celebrating a different aspect of Scottish culture. The Edinburgh International Book Festival brings together writers and readers from around the world, while the Edinburgh Jazz & Blues Festival fills the city's streets with the sounds of soulful music. The Edinburgh Science Festival offers a fascinating exploration of scientific discovery, and the Edinburgh Film Festival showcases the best of independent and international cinema. The city's festival scene is a testament to its vibrant and diverse cultural landscape, a place where artistic expression thrives in all its forms.

Scotland's cultural heritage is also deeply rooted in its traditional music and dance. Ceilidhs, lively gatherings featuring traditional Scottish music and dancing, are a staple of Scottish social life. These events are not just performances; they're participatory experiences, where everyone is encouraged to join in the fun. The music, a blend of traditional instruments like the fiddle, accordion, and bagpipes, creates a vibrant and infectious atmosphere. The dances, from the energetic reels to the graceful strathspeys, are a celebration of Scottish heritage and community spirit. You can find ceilidhs in pubs, community halls, and even castles, each offering a unique and authentic experience.

Beyond the ceilidh, Scotland's cultural landscape is rich in other forms of artistic expression. Local crafts, from handwoven textiles and intricate jewelry to hand-carved wooden sculptures and pottery, showcase the skill and creativity of Scottish artisans. You can explore craft shops and galleries in towns and villages across the country, discovering unique and beautiful pieces that reflect the region's artistic traditions. Many locations hold craft fairs, and art shows, especially during the summer months.

- **Getting to Edinburgh from within Scotland:** Edinburgh is well-connected by train and bus services from other major Scottish cities like Glasgow, Aberdeen, and Inverness.
- **Things to do in Edinburgh:** Beyond the festivals and cultural experiences, explore the city's historic landmarks, such as Edinburgh Castle and the Royal Mile, hike Arthur's Seat, and enjoy the vibrant nightlife.

- Where to stay in Edinburgh: Edinburgh offers a wide range of accommodation options, from luxury hotels and boutique guesthouses to budget-friendly hostels and apartments.
- **Food and beverages in Edinburgh:** Enjoy traditional Scottish fare at local pubs, sample fresh seafood at coastal restaurants, and explore the city's thriving craft beer and whisky scene.

Scotland's artistic expressions are not just relics of the past; they are living traditions, constantly evolving and adapting to the present. They are a testament to the creativity and resilience of the Scottish people, a celebration of their cultural heritage, and a vibrant expression of their identity.

SCOTLAND

CHAPTER 8
HIDDEN GEMS & QUIRKY FINDS

The map was a scrap of paper, stained with whisky and scribbled with cryptic symbols, a gift from a grizzled old fisherman in a remote Hebridean pub. He'd leaned close, his breath smelling of peat and the sea, and whispered, "Follow the standing stones that sing to the seals. You'll find what you're looking for." I'd dismissed it as the ramblings of a local eccentric, another tall tale spun over a dram or two. But something about his eyes, the intensity in his gaze, had stayed with me.

Days later, I found myself on the windswept shores of a tiny island, the map clutched in my hand, the wind whipping at my coat. The standing stones, a circle of weathered monoliths, stood silhouetted against the stormy sky. As the tide receded, a strange, haunting melody filled the air, a chorus of seal calls that seemed to emanate from the stones themselves. It was an eerie, otherworldly sound, a whisper from a forgotten time.

And then, I saw it. A small, hidden cave, its entrance obscured by seaweed and barnacles. Inside, a collection of objects lay scattered on the damp sand: a rusted compass, a faded photograph of a sailing ship, a small, intricately carved wooden box. It was a treasure trove of forgotten memories, a glimpse into the lives of those who had once called this remote island home.

This experience, this sense of discovery, this feeling of stumbling upon something truly unique, is what I want to share with you. Scotland is a land of hidden gems, of quirky finds and unexpected delights. Beyond the well-trodden tourist trails, there are countless places waiting to be discovered, each with its own story to tell.

- **The Lost Village of St. Kilda:** This remote archipelago, abandoned in 1930, is a haunting reminder of a way of life that has vanished. The stark beauty of the islands, the abandoned village, and the towering sea cliffs create a sense of isolation and wonder. Its history is both tragic and compelling, and the bird life is world renowned.
- **Fossil Hunting on the Isle of Skye:** Skye's rugged coastline is a treasure trove of fossils, a window into the ancient world. Arm yourself with a map and a keen eye, and you might discover the remains of dinosaurs, ammonites, and other prehistoric creatures.

- **The Mysterious Rosslyn Chapel:** This 15th-century chapel, with its intricate carvings and cryptic symbols, has long been shrouded in mystery. Its connection to the Knights Templar and the Holy Grail has fueled countless theories and legends. The sheer volume of the carvings makes this a must see for anyone interested in history, or art.
- **The Paper Cave of Smo**o: Deep within a sea cave near Durness, a hidden chamber holds a collection of messages and drawings left by visitors over the centuries. It's a quirky and unique way to connect with the history of the area.
- **The Whaligoe Steps:** These 365 steps, carved into the cliffs near Wick, lead down to a hidden harbor, once a bustling fishing village. The dramatic scenery and the sense of isolation make this a truly unforgettable experience. The climb back up is also quite the work out
    - **The Fairy Glen on Skye**: This enchanting landscape, with its conical hills and winding paths, feels like a scene from a fairy tale. It's a place where imagination takes flight, and where ..

the boundaries between reality and fantasy blur
- **The Corrieshalloch Gorge:** A hidden gorge with a suspension bridge, and a waterfall, this location is a breathtaking display of natural beauty. The sheer power of the falls, and the depth of the gorge, make this a very memorable experience.
- **Local Festivals** and Gatherings: Beyond the major events, seek out the smaller, more intimate gatherings that celebrate local traditions and customs. These hidden gems often offer the most authentic and memorable experiences.

Scotland's hidden gems are not just places to see; they are experiences to be savored, memories to be made. They are a reminder that even in a world that often feels predictable, there are still places of mystery and wonder waiting to be discovered. Edinburgh, a city of elegant facades and historic grandeur, holds a dark and intriguing secret beneath its cobblestone streets. The underground vaults, a network of hidden chambers and alleyways, offer a glimpse into a forgotten world, a world of poverty, crime, and ghostly tales. These subterranean spaces, once bustling with life, now echo with the whispers of the past, their damp walls holding the secrets of centuries. Exploring these vaults is not merely a historical tour; it's a descent into the city's shadow self, a journey into the heart of its most haunting stories. Guided tours, often led by storytellers with a flair for the dramatic, reveal the tales of the city's forgotten inhabitants: the criminals, the paupers, and the victims of plague. The atmosphere is thick with history, the air heavy with the weight of the past. You don't just observe; you feel the city's dark history.

Beyond the ghostly tales and subterranean depths, Edinburgh also offers pockets of tranquility, hidden oases amidst the urban bustle. Secret gardens, tucked away behind high walls

and wrought-iron gates, offer a respite from the city's frenetic energy. These green spaces, often overlooked by tourists, provide a sanctuary for contemplation and relaxation. You'll find meticulously manicured gardens, wild and untamed green spaces, and hidden courtyards, each offering a unique and peaceful escape. The Physic Garden, for example, is a haven of medicinal plants and fragrant herbs, a place where you can reconnect with nature and find a moment of calm. The Dean Village, a peaceful and historic area, offers a walk along the Water of Leith, a peaceful river that runs through the city. These hidden gardens and urban oases are a testament to Edinburgh's ability to balance its historic charm with its modern vibrancy, offering both adventure and tranquility.

Edinburgh's shopping scene is as unique and diverse as its cultural landscape. Beyond the high-street chains and tourist traps, you'll find a wealth of independent boutiques and unique shops, offering a curated selection of local crafts, artisan goods, and vintage treasures. The Grassmarket, a historic marketplace, is home to a collection of independent shops selling everything from handcrafted jewelry and Scottish textiles to vintage clothing and antique maps. Victoria Street, with its colorful facades and winding cobblestones, is a haven for quirky boutiques and independent bookshops. The area around the Royal Mile contains many small shops selling high quality Scottish goods. From hand made kilts, to unique pieces of Scottish jewelry, the area is a must see for shoppers.

- **Getting to Edinburgh from within the UK**: Edinburgh is well-connected by train and bus services from other major UK cities like London, Manchester, and Birmingham.
- **Things to do in Edinburgh**: Beyond the underground vaults, secret gardens, and unique shops, explore the city's historic landmarks, such as Edinburgh Castle and the Royal Mile, hike Arthur's Seat, and enjoy the vibrant nightlife.
- **Where to stay in Edinburgh**: Edinburgh offers a wide range of accommodation options, from luxury hotels and boutique guesthouses to budget-friendly hostels and1 apartments.
- **Food and beverages in Edinburgh:** Enjoy traditional Scottish fare at local pubs, sample fresh seafood at coastal restaurants, and explore the city's thriving craft beer and whisky scene.

Edinburgh's hidden gems, whether they be its dark underground vaults, its tranquil secret gardens, or its unique shops, offer a glimpse into the city's multifaceted character. They are a reminder that even in a city steeped in history, there are always new and unexpected discoveries to be made.

SCOTLAND WONDERS

CHAPTER 9
EXPLORING SCOTLAND'S NATURAL WONDERS

The salt spray stung my face, the wind a relentless force that whipped at my waterproofs. I clung to the railing of the small ferry, the churning waves a dark, restless expanse beneath us. We were heading to Staffa, a tiny, uninhabited island in the Inner Hebrides, a place I'd only seen in grainy photographs, a place rumored to hold a secret whispered in basalt and sea spray. The journey itself had been a pilgrimage, a series of winding roads and choppy boat rides, each leg adding to the sense of isolation, the feeling of venturing to the edge of the world.

The island rose from the sea like a forgotten fortress, its basalt columns a stark, geometric masterpiece, a testament to the raw power of volcanic forces. But it wasn't the columns themselves that drew me, it was the cave. Fingal's Cave. A natural cathedral, carved by the sea, its echoing chambers filled with the roar of the waves, a sound that resonated deep within my soul.

I'd read the stories, the legends of giants and magic, the tales of musicians inspired by the cave's haunting acoustics. But standing there, on the threshold of this natural wonder, the legends seemed to fade, replaced by a sense of awe, a profound connection to the raw, untamed beauty of the natural world. The cave wasn't just a geological formation; it was a living, breathing entity, a testament to the power of nature to create art on a scale that dwarfed human imagination.

This experience, this sense of wonder, this feeling of being humbled by the sheer majesty of the natural world, is what I want to share with you. Scotland is a land of breathtaking natural wonders, a place where the landscapes are as dramatic as the legends they inspire. From the towering peaks of the Highlands to the windswept shores of the islands, Scotland's natural beauty is a force to be reckoned with.

- **The Majesty of the Highlands:** The Highlands are a vast wilderness, a tapestry of mountains, glens, and lochs. Drive the North Coast 500, a scenic route that winds its way along the coast, offering panoramic views of some of the most dramatic landscapes in Europe. Hike the trails of the Cairngorms National Park, explore the depths of Loch Ness, and witness the raw beauty of Glencoe.
- **The Enchanting Isle of Skye**: Skye is a land of jagged peaks, crystal-clear pools, and dramatic coastlines. Hike the Old Man of Storr, explore the Fairy Pools, and witness the Quiraing, a landscape that seems to belong in a fantasy novel. The light on Skye, ever changing, adds to the magical feeling of the island.
- **The Wild Beauty of the Islands:** Scotland's islands, from the Outer Hebrides to the Shetland Islands, offer a unique and unforgettable experience. Explore the ancient standing stones of the Callanish Stones, witness the puffins nesting on the Isle of May, and experience the remote beauty of St. Kilda. The islands are a place where the rhythms of life are dictated by the tides and the seasons.
- **The Coastal Wonders:** Scotland's coastline is a masterpiece of natural beauty, with towering cliffs, secluded beaches, and hidden coves. Explore the sea caves of Smoo, witness the seabird colonies of the Bass Rock, and walk the windswept beaches of the Outer Hebrides. The contrast of the dark rock, against the white sand beaches, is something

that must be seen.
- **The Ancient Forests:** The remnants of the Caledonian Forest, Scotland's ancient woodland, offer a glimpse into a lost world. Explore the forests of Glen Affric, where ancient Scots pine trees stand tall, and witness the wildlife that calls these forests home.
- The Northern Lights: In the far north of Scotland, the aurora borealis, or Northern Lights, dances across the night sky, a breathtaking display of natural wonder. The winter months offer the best chance to witness this celestial spectacle.
- The Wildlife Encounters: Scotland is home to a diverse array of wildlife, from red deer and golden eagles to dolphins and whales. Take a wildlife watching tour, and you might encounter these magnificent creatures in their natural habitat.

Scotland's natural wonders are not just places to visit; they are experiences to be savored, memories to be made. They are a reminder of the power and beauty of the natural world, a testament to the raw, untamed spirit of Scotland.

Edinburgh, a city etched in history and crowned by dramatic landscapes, offers a unique opportunity to witness its beauty from above. Arthur's Seat, an ancient volcano rising from the heart of the city, provides panoramic views that stretch across the rooftops, over the Firth of Forth, and into the rolling hills beyond. The climb, a rewarding ascent, reveals the city's intricate layout, its historic Old Town juxtaposed against the modern skyline. The wind, a constant companion, carries the sounds of the city, a low hum of activity that fades into the distance. Calton Hill, another iconic vantage point, offers a different perspective, showcasing the city's architectural grandeur. The neoclassical monuments, standing like sentinels against the sky, frame the cityscape, creating a picture-perfect anorama. These elevated viewpoints are not just about the views; they are about gaining a sense of place, understanding the city's geography, and appreciating its unique blend of urban and natural landscapes.

Beyond the city's immediate boundaries, Scotland beckons with its vast network of scenic walks and hiking trails. The country's diverse terrain, from the rugged Highlands to the gentle Lowlands, offers trails for every level of adventurer. You can wander through ancient forests, follow winding river paths, and ascend towering mountains, each trail revealing a different facet of Scotland's natural beauty. The West Highland Way, a long-distance trail that stretches from Milngavie to Fort William, is a classic Scottish hiking experience, offering breathtaking views of lochs, mountains, and glens. The Fife Coastal Path, a scenic route that hugs the coastline, reveals hidden coves, sandy beaches, and charming fishing villages. These trails are not just about physical exertion; they are about immersing oneself in the Scottish landscape, connecting with nature, and experiencing the country's raw, untamed beauty.

Scotland's coastline, a dramatic interplay of cliffs, beaches, and sea life, offers a wealth of coastal adventures. From the windswept shores of the Outer Hebrides to the sheltered coves of the East Neuk of Fife, the coastline is a playground for explorers. You can kayak through sea caves, explore hidden beaches, and witness the spectacle of seabird colonies. The Isle of Mull, with its rugged coastline and abundant wildlife, is a haven for nature lovers. You can spot dolphins, whales, and seals, and explore the island's ancient forests and dramatic cliffs. The beaches of the Outer Hebrides, with their pristine white sand and turquoise waters, offer a sense of isolation and tranquility. These coastal adventures are not just about

adrenaline; they are about experiencing the raw power of the sea, connecting with the marine environment, and appreciating the delicate balance of coastal ecosystems.

- **Getting to Edinburgh from Europe:** Edinburgh Airport offers direct flights from many major European cities. The city is also easily accessible by train from London and other UK cities.
- **Things to do in Edinburgh:** Beyond the panoramic views and outdoor activities, explore the city's historic landmarks, such as Edinburgh Castle and the Royal Mile, visit the National Museum of Scotland, and enjoy the vibrant arts and culture scene.
- **Where to stay in Edinburgh:** Edinburgh offers a wide range of accommodation options, from luxury hotels and boutique guesthouses to budget-friendly hostels and apartments.
- **Food and beverages in Edinburgh:** Enjoy traditional Scottish fare at local pubs, sample fresh seafood at coastal restaurants, and explore the city's thriving craft beer and whisky scene.

Scotland's natural landscapes, from its panoramic city views to its scenic trails and coastal adventures, offer a profound connection to the country's raw, untamed beauty. They are a reminder of the power and majesty of the natural world, and an invitation to explore the diverse and captivating landscapes that make Scotland so unique.

CHAPTER 10

RESPONSIBLE TRAVEL & LASTING MEMORIES

The fire crackled, casting dancing shadows on the rough stone walls of the bothy. Outside, the wind howled, a constant reminder of the wildness that surrounded us. I'd spent the day volunteering on a remote island, helping to restore a section of the coastal path, a task that seemed insignificant against the vastness of the landscape. But as I sat by the fire, listening to the islanders tell stories of their connection to the land, I understood the importance of our efforts. It wasn't just about the path; it was about preserving a way of life, a delicate balance between human activity and the natural world.

I'd arrived in Scotland with a desire to explore its beauty, to experience its landscapes and culture. But as I traveled, I began to realize the impact of tourism, the delicate balance between sharing a place and preserving it. The overflowing bins in popular tourist spots, the erosion of fragile ecosystems, the subtle shifts in local culture – these were not just abstract concepts; they were real, tangible consequences of our presence.

That night, in the warmth of the bothy, I made a promise to myself: to travel differently, to leave a positive impact, to create lasting memories that were not just mine, but also those of the places I visited. It wasn't about grand gestures or heroic acts; it was about small, conscious choices, about being mindful of my footprint, about respecting the land and its people.

This commitment to responsible travel, this desire to create lasting memories that benefit both the traveler and the destination, is what I want to share with you. Scotland is a land of extraordinary beauty and cultural richness, a place that deserves our respect and care.

- **Embrace Sustainable Practices**: Choose eco-friendly accommodations, support local businesses that prioritize sustainability, and minimize your waste. Pack reusable water bottles, shopping bags, and food containers. Opt for public transportation, walking, or cycling whenever possible.
- **Respect Local Cultures:** Learn about the customs and traditions of the places you visit. Be mindful of local sensitivities, and avoid behaviors that could be considered disrespectful. Support local artisans and craftspeople by purchasing their products directly.
- **Protect Natural Environments:** Stay on designated trails, avoid disturbing wildlife, and dispose of waste responsibly. Participate in local conservation efforts, such as beach cleanups or tree planting initiatives.
- **Support Local Economies:** Choose locally owned restaurants, shops, and tour operators. Buy local produce and products, and contribute to the economic well-being of the communities you visit.
- **Engage in Meaningful Experiences**: Seek out opportunities to connect with local people and learn about their way of life. Participate in cultural events, volunteer with local organizations, and engage in responsible wildlife tourism.
- **Minimize Your Carbon Footprint**: Offset your carbon emissions by supporting carbon reduction projects. Choose transportation options with lower carbon emissions, and reduce your energy consumption while traveling.

- Leave No Trace: Follow the principles of Leave No Trace, which emphasize minimizing your impact on the environment. Pack out what you pack in, avoid disturbing natural features, and respect wildlife.
- Travel During Off-Peak Seasons: Consider traveling during the shoulder or off-season to avoid crowds and reduce pressure on popular destinations. This can also provide a more authentic and immersive travel experience.
- Educate Yourself: Learn about the environmental and cultural challenges facing the places you visit. This knowledge will help you make informed decisions and contribute to responsible travel practices.
- Share Your Experiences Responsibly: Encourage others to travel responsibly by sharing your experiences and insights. Use social media to promote sustainable tourism and raise awareness about responsible travel practices.

Scotland offers a unique opportunity to create lasting memories that are both meaningful and responsible. By embracing sustainable practices, respecting local cultures, and protecting natural environments, we can ensure that future generations will also have the opportunity to experience the magic of this extraordinary land.

Scotland's allure lies not just in its dramatic landscapes and rich history, but also in the delicate balance between its natural beauty and the communities that call it home. Sustainable tourism is not a trend here; it's a responsibility, a way to ensure that the magic of Scotland endures for generations to come. It's about more than just reducing your carbon footprint; it's about actively contributing to the well-being of the places you visit. Choosing locally owned accommodations, dining at restaurants that source their ingredients from nearby farms, and supporting artisans who create nique, handcrafted goods –

these are not just ethical choices, they are ways to experience the authentic heart of Scotland. It's about respecting the land, understanding its rhythms, and appreciating the interconnectedness of all living things. When you walk the ancient trails, leave no trace. When you encounter wildlife, observe from a distance, allowing them to thrive in their natural habitat. When you engage with local communities, listen to their stories, learn about their traditions, and contribute to their economic vitality. This approach to travel transforms a mere visit into a meaningful exchange, a way to create lasting memories that benefit both the traveler and the destination.

Capturing the essence of Scotland, the fleeting moments of beauty and wonder, is an art in itself. Photography and travel journaling are not just about documenting your journey; they are about preserving the emotions, the sensations, and the stories that make your experience unique. When you frame a shot of the Highlands, don't just capture the mountains; capture the light, the mist, the feeling of standing on the edge of the world. When you write in your journal, don't just list the places you visited; describe the sounds, the smells, the tastes, the conversations that shaped your experience. Seek out the hidden details, the subtle nuances, the moments that might otherwise go unnoticed. Talk to locals, ask them about their lives, their traditions, their favorite places. Their stories will add depth and richness to your memories. Use your photographs to tell a story, to evoke a feeling, to transport yourself back to that moment in time. Use your journal to reflect on your experiences, to process your emotions, to deepen your understanding of the places you visited. These tools are not just for recording; they are for remembering, for reliving, for sharing the magic of Scotland with others.

As your Scottish adventure draws to a close, the thought of returning begins to take root. Scotland has a way of capturing your heart, of leaving you with a longing to explore its hidden corners and delve deeper into its rich tapestry of culture and history. Planning your return is not just about scheduling another trip; it's about continuing a journey, about deepening your connection to a land that has become a part of you.Consider exploring the regions you missed, venturing to the remote islands, or immersing yourself in the local festivals and traditions. Research the hidden gems, the lesser-known trails, the local events that offer a more authentic experience. Talk to locals, ask them for recommendations, and discover the places they cherish. Consider a longer stay, allowing yourself time to truly immerse yourself in the Scottish way of life. Learn a few phrases of Gaelic, try your hand at traditional crafts, or volunteer with a local conservation project.

- Getting to Edinburgh from North America: Edinburgh Airport offers direct flights from several major North American cities. Plan your trip during the summer months to enjoy longer daylight hours and warmer weather.
- Things to do in Edinburgh: Beyond the iconic landmarks, explore the city's hidden alleyways, visit the independent shops, and attend a traditional ceilidh. Consider a day trip to the nearby Pentland Hills for hiking and scenic views.
- Where to stay in Edinburgh: Consider staying in a locally owned guesthouse or apartment to support the local economy and experience a more authentic Scottish atmosphere.
- Food and beverages in Edinburgh: Sample traditional Scottish dishes at local pubs, try the craft beers at a local brewery, and indulge in a whisky tasting at a traditional whisky bar.

Scotland is a land of endless discovery, a place where every visit reveals new layers of beauty and wonder. Planning your return is not just about revisiting a destination; it's about continuing a love affair, about deepening your appreciation for a land that has captured your soul.

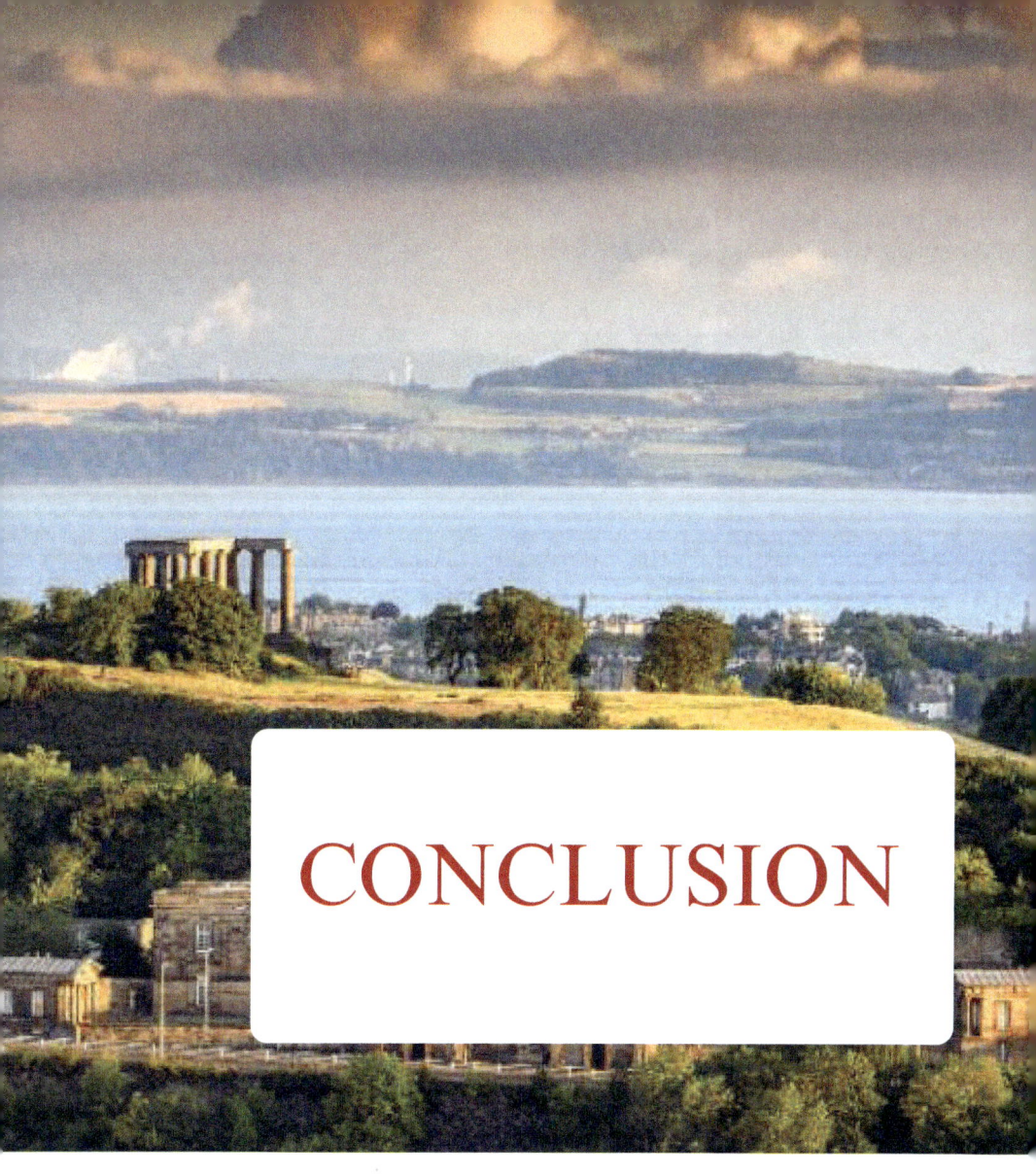

CONCLUSION

And so, our journey through the heart of Scotland draws to a close. But, truly, it's not an ending at all, is it? It's a beginning. A beginning of your own adventure, a personal exploration of a land that whispers secrets in the wind and paints stories across its landscapes. This book, I hope, hasn't just been a guide; it's been a companion, a hand extended, a nudge toward the hidden corners and the heartfelt experiences that make Scotland so profoundly unforgettable.

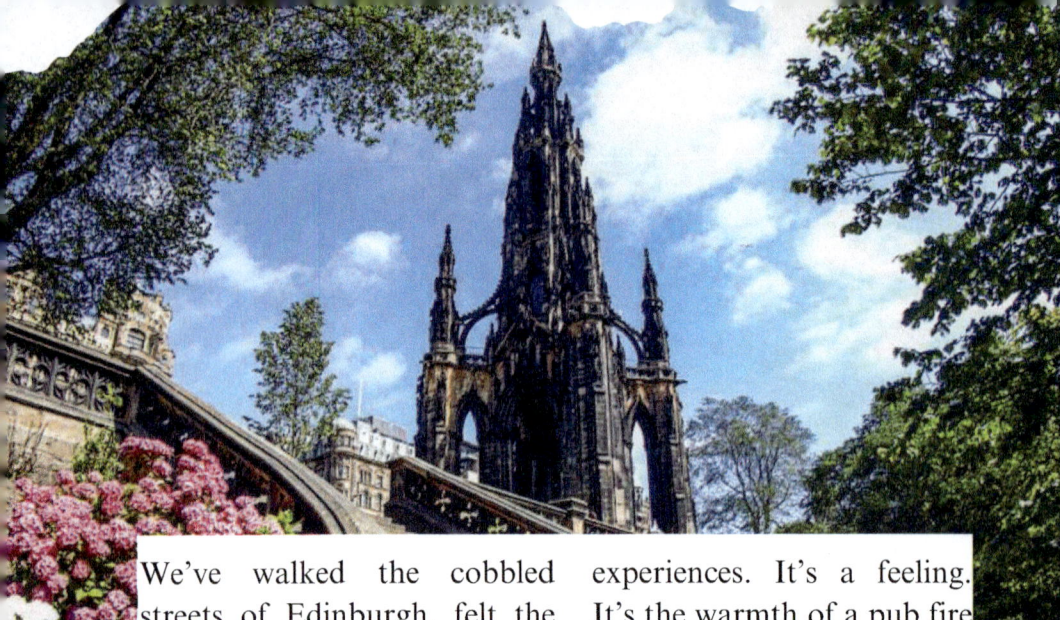

We've walked the cobbled streets of Edinburgh, felt the raw energy of its festivals, and tasted the soul of Scottish cuisine. We've ventured into the Highlands, where mountains pierce the sky and lochs hold ancient mysteries, and we've journeyed to the islands, where the sea shapes the land and the wind carries tales of Vikings and fairies. We've explored the whispers of history in ancient stones, and felt the pulse of modern Scotland in its vibrant cities. We've considered the importance of leaving a positive impact, ensuring this incredible place remains for others to experience.

But Scotland is more than just a collection of sights and experiences. It's a feeling. It's the warmth of a pub fire on a cold winter's night, the sound of bagpipes echoing through a glen, the taste of whisky warmed by peat smoke, the kindness in a stranger's eyes, and the sheer, breathtaking beauty of a landscape that leaves you speechless.

Go, then. Go and discover your own Scotland. Wander the hidden paths, listen to the stories whispered by the wind, and let the magic of this land seep into your soul. Capture the fleeting moments, the unexpected encounters, the feelings that resonate deep within. And when you return, share your stories, not just as a tourist,

but as a fellow traveler, a friend of Scotland.
Because Scotland, once experienced, stays with you. It becomes a part of you, a memory etched in your heart, a longing for the day you return. And you will return You'll feel the pull of the mountains, the call of the sea, the warmth of the people. And when you do, you'll discover that Scotland, like any good story, has many chapters yet to be written. And you, my friend, are now a part of that story.
.

ESSENTIAL MAPS

EDINBURGH

SCAN THE QR CODE

1. Open your device camera app.
2. Point the camera at the QR code.
3. Ensure the camera code is within the frame and well-lit.
4. Wait for your device to recognize the QR code.
5. Once recognized, tap on the notification or follow the prompt to access the content or action associated with the QR code.

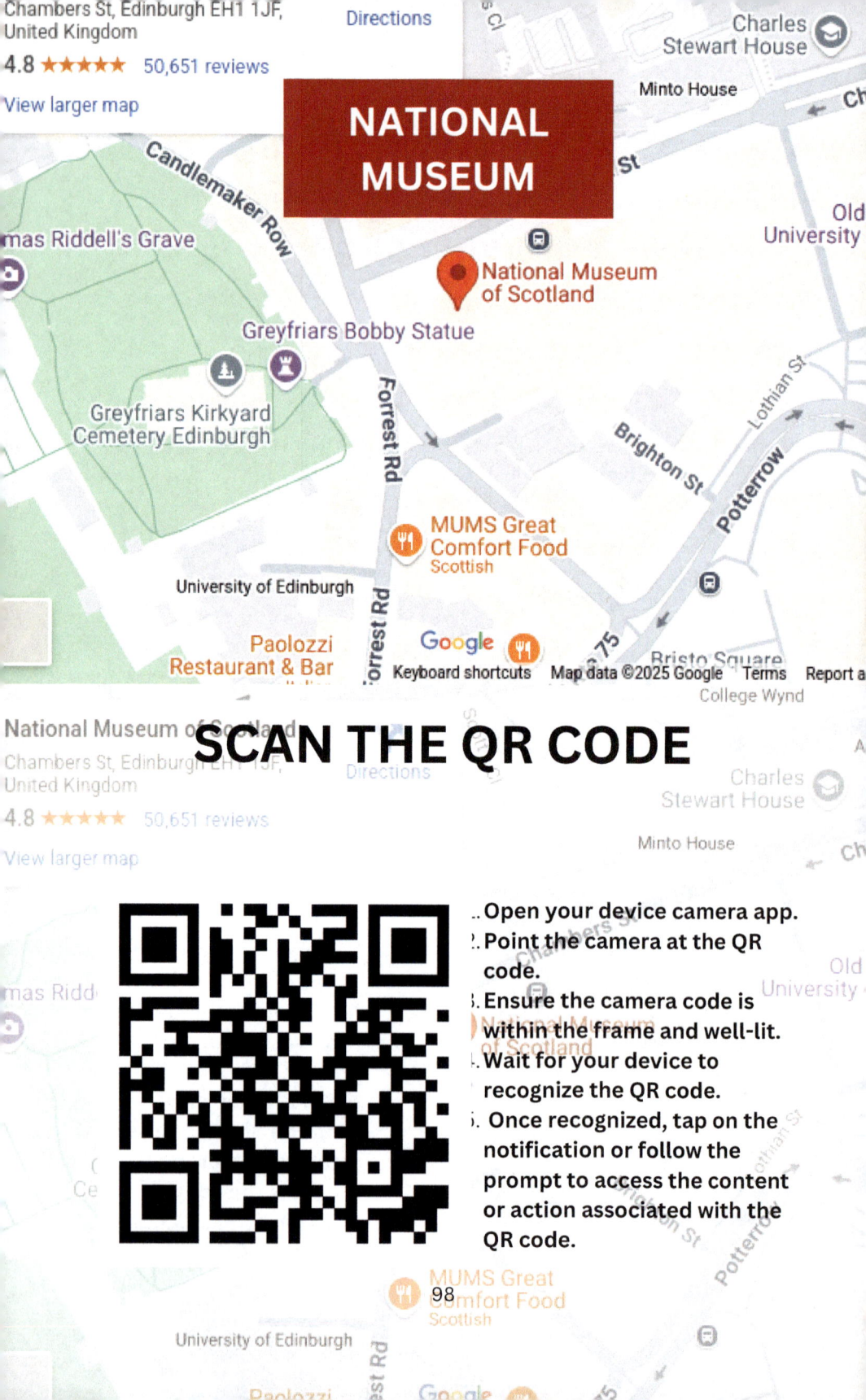

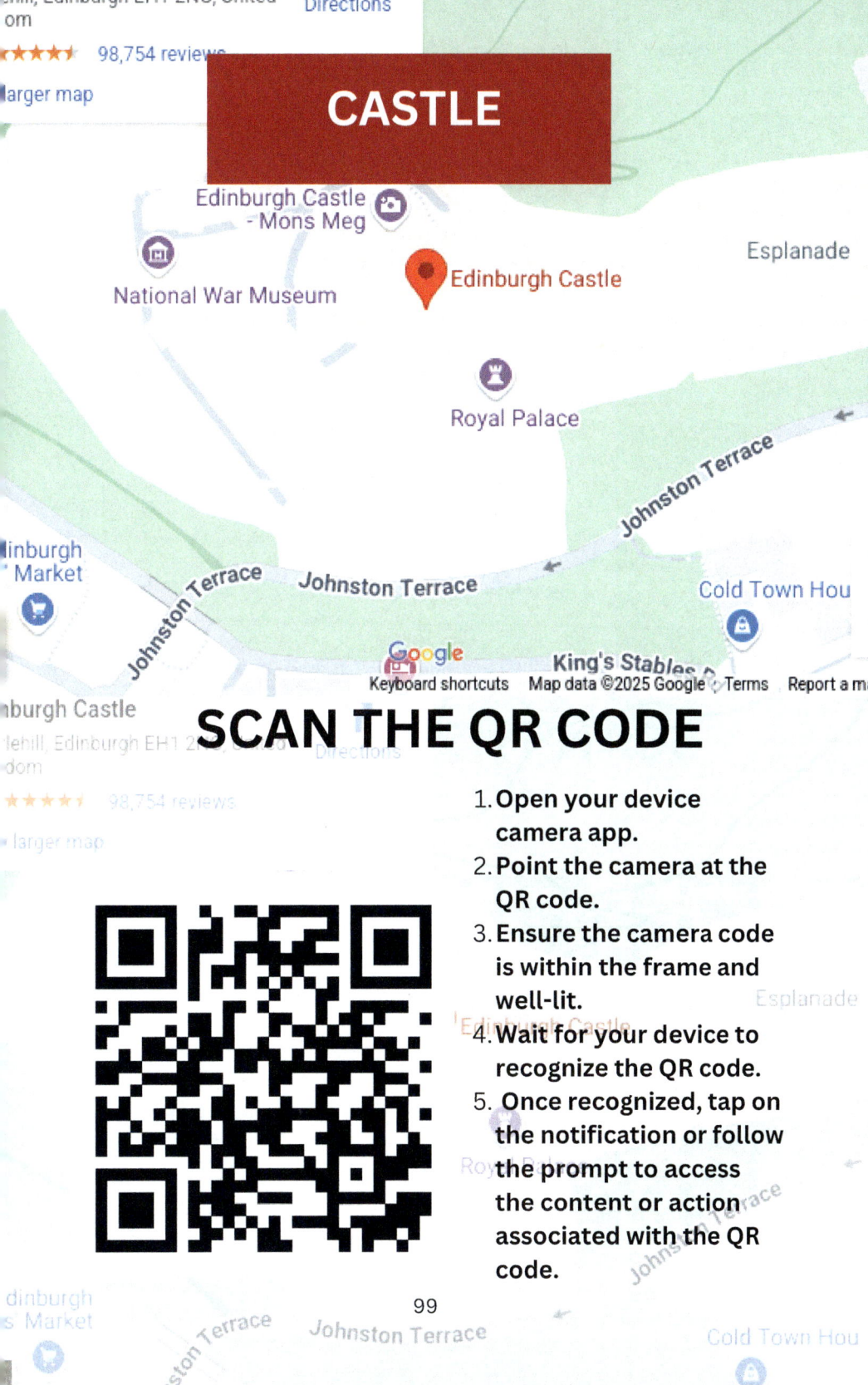

CASTLE

SCAN THE QR CODE

1. Open your device camera app.
2. Point the camera at the QR code.
3. Ensure the camera code is within the frame and well-lit.
4. Wait for your device to recognize the QR code.
5. Once recognized, tap on the notification or follow the prompt to access the content or action associated with the QR code.

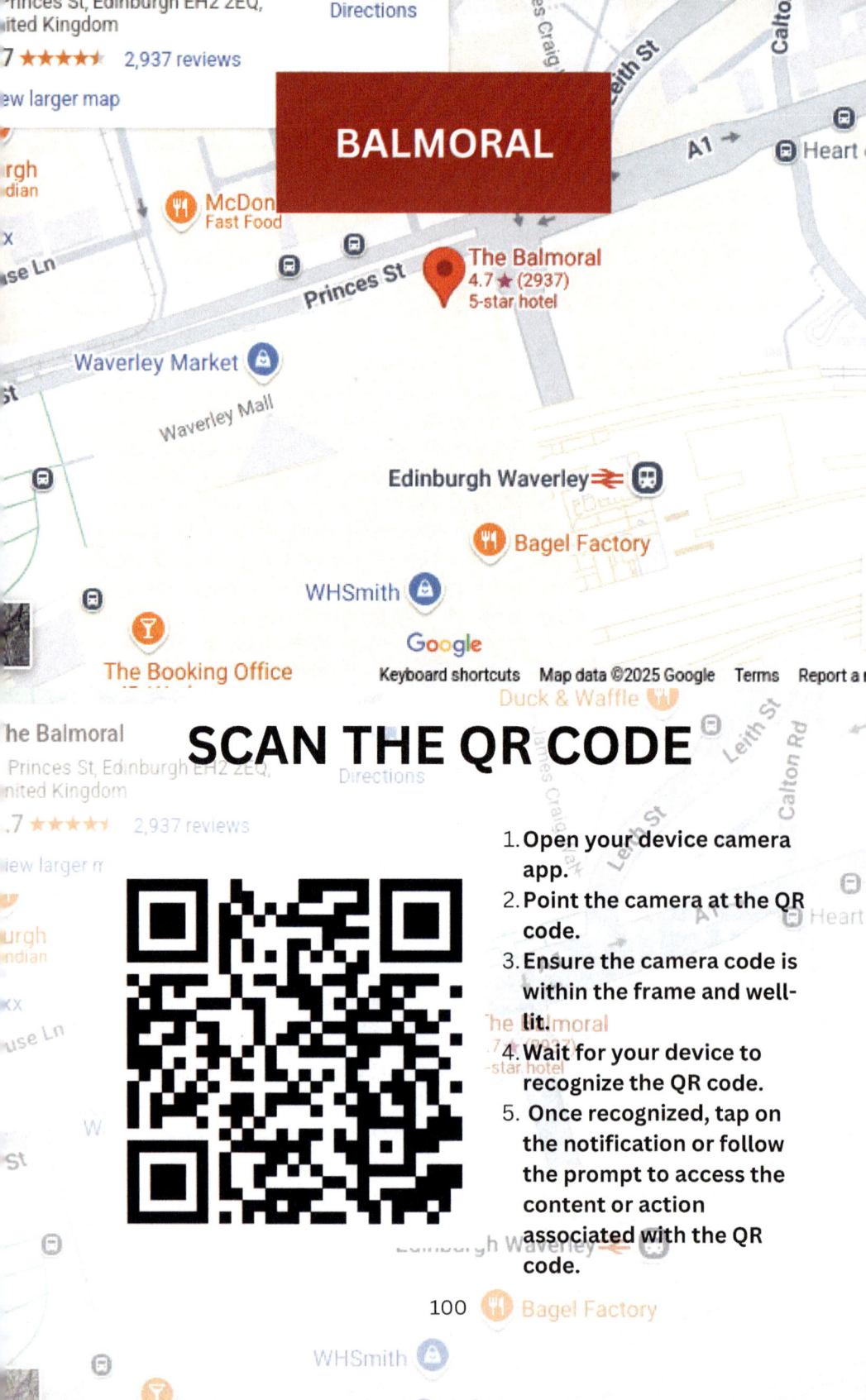

Printed in Dunstable, United Kingdom